Crocheted Finger Puppets

Crocheted Finger Puppets

GINA ALTON

GUILD OF MASTER
CRAFTSMAN PUBLICATIONS

First published 2009 by
Guild of Master Craftsman Publications Ltd
Castle Place, 166 High Street,
Lewes, East Sussex BN7 1XU

Reprinted 2010 (twice)

ISBN: 978-1-86108-657-0

A catalogue record of this book is available from the
British Library.

Associate Publisher: Jonathan Bailey
Production Manager: Jim Bulley
Managing Editor: Gerrie Purcell
Senior Project Editor: Virginia Brehaut
Managing Art Editor: Gilda Pacitti
Designer: Jo Patterson

Set in Gill Sans and Ribbon

Colour origination by **GMC Reprographics**
Printed and bound in Thailand by KNP

Why we love finger puppets

Crocheted finger puppets are quick and easy to create, excellent as little gifts and fun for all ages. They can amuse tiny tots, decorate your desk, become action characters in bedtime stories or adorn your computer monitor. They are small, lightweight, totally portable and ideal for using up some of your yarn stash.

I started making little puppets to amuse my children during long waits at the doctor's office, while travelling abroad and as a distraction from those 'terrible-twos' tantrums! They began as very simple shapes, and over the years evolved into the more detailed puppet sets featured in this book. This evolution was fuelled by a never-ending stream of inspiration from my children, who asked for ever better and more complex toys to play with.

You can use these patterns as a starting point for your own creations, or follow them to the letter if you like. The designs are intended to be whimsical, silly, entertaining and inspiring. If you've never attempted crochet before you might like to start with the Bumble Bees or Wormhole Worms! If you are a more experienced crocheter maybe you'd prefer to try making Marianna the Mermaid or our hero, SuperFred the Shape-shifter. But whatever you do, have fun!

Contents

In the wild

Under the sea

In outer space

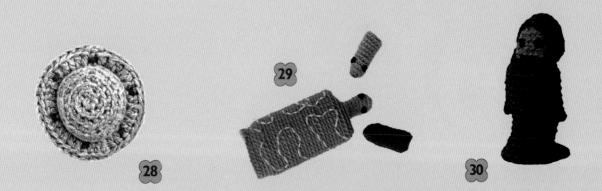

In the wild

Mr Monkey is all set for the office, with his packed lunch – a bunch of bananas – and his briefcase (just the thing for monkey business). Make him a monkey friend and they can go wild at the weekend!

Monkey

Materials

- Any DK yarn in dark brown, tan and white for monkey, black for briefcase and yellow for bananas
- 3.25mm (USD/3, UK10) and 3.5mm (USE/4, UK9) hooks
- Darning needle and scissors

Method

Monkey: The puppet base is made by starting at the top of the head and working down for the body. The limbs and tail are then worked separately and added on, as are the facial features.

Bananas: The bunch of bananas is formed by first working a single row in slip stitch for each banana, then gathering them together at the joined end to group them into a bunch.

Briefcase: This is simply a rectangle worked in rows of double crochet, with a round of edging finishing with a chain stitch handle.

For further guidance, see the outer body and googly eyes stitch diagrams on page 151.

Monkey

Work in spiral TBLs throughout head, neck and body.

Head

With 3.5mm hook and dark brown yarn, mk floop and 1ch.

Rnd 1: 6dc into floop. 6 sts.
Rnd 2: Dc2inc 6 times. 12 sts.
Rnd 3: (1dc, dc2inc) 6 times. 18 sts.
Rnds 4–6: Wk even in dc.
Rnd 7: (1dc, dc2tog) 6 times. 12 sts.

Neck

Rnds 8-9: Wk even in ss.

Body

Rnds 10–18: Wk even in dc.
Fasten off.

Arms (make 2)

With 3.5mm hook and dark brown yarn, mk sl-knot and 12ch.
Row 1: Sk1ch, ss to end.
Fasten off, leaving a tail for sewing onto body.

Hands (make 2)

Work in spiral TBLs.
With 3.5mm hook and tan yarn, mk floop and 1 ch.
Rnd 1: 7dc into floop. 7 sts.
Rnds 2–3: Wk even in dc.
Fasten off and sew hand to arm. Sew arm in place on body.

Legs (make 2)

With 3.5mm hook and dark brown yarn, mk sl-knot and 15ch.
Row 1: Sk1ch, ss to end.
Fasten off, leaving a tail for sewing onto body.

Feet (make 2)

Work in spiral TBLs.
With 3.5mm hook and tan yarn, mk floop and 1 ch.
Rnd 1: 8dc into floop. 8 sts.
Rnds 2–3: Wk even in dc.
Fasten off and sew foot to leg. Sew leg in place on body.

Tail

With 3.5mm hook and dark brown yarn, mk sl-knot and 30ch.
Row 1: Wk (1ss in every second ch st) 10 times, then 1ss in each ch st to end.
Fasten off and sew into place on body.

Face

With 3.5mm hook and tan yarn, mk floop and 1ch.
Rnd 1: 6dc into floop. 6 sts.
Rnd 2: Dc2inc 6 times. 12 sts.
Rnd 3: 1dc, (1dc, dc2inc) 3 times (this is the mouth area), * 1ss, (1dc, 1htr, 1dc) in next st (this is the eye backing), rep from * once, 1ss.
Fasten off.

Eyes (make 2)

With 3.25mm hook and white yarn, mk floop and 1ch.

Rnd 1: 6dc into floop. 6 sts.

Ss to join, and fasten off. Sew in beg end of yarn to WS of eye.

Ears (make 2)

With 3.5mm hook and dark brown yarn, mk floop and 1ch.

Rnd 1: 6dc into floop. 6 sts.

Rnd 2: Wk even in ss (a little loosely). Fasten off leaving a tail for sewing, and sew ears onto either side of head.

Tufts

With 3.5mm hook and dark brown yarn, mk sl-knot.

Wk (4ch, sk1ch, 3ss) 4 times. Fasten off leaving a tail for sewing, and sew onto top of head.

Finishing

With a darning needle and dark brown yarn, stitch pupils onto the eyes and a nose and mouth onto the face. Sew eyes onto the face using mattress stitch, then sew face onto the head.

Bananas

With 3.5mm hook and yellow yarn, mk sl-knot, (7ch, sk1ch, 6ss) 7 times. 7 bananas.

Now dc7tog, and fasten off leaving a 6in (15cm) tail for sewing.

Finishing

With a darning needle, gather tog the bananas into a bunch, making looping sts to form a stalk.

Variations

For a wilder-looking monkey, sew the eyes on a bit askew... and lose the briefcase!

Briefcase

Wk TFBLs throughout.

With 3.5mm hook and black yarn, mk sl-knot and 8ch.

Row 1: Sk1ch, 6dc. 6 sts.

Rows 2–7: 1ch, 6dc.

Now wk one rnd of dc edging on three sides, working (1dc, 1ch, 1dc) into each corner.

To form a 'handle', wk (2ss, mk4ch and sk 2 sts, 2ss) along fourth side.

Finishing

Fasten off and sew in any loose ends. Steam press so that it lies flat nicely.

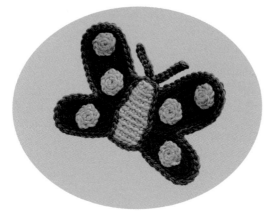

Betsy and Boopsie the beautiful butterflies flutter around all day;
then when the day is done they can snuggle down in their own
flowery pink bags for the night.

Butterflies

Materials

- Any DK yarn in light pink, dark pink and light purple
  for both butterflies and bags
- 3.5mm (USE/4, UK9) hook
- Darning needle and scissors

*For further guidance, see the butterfly stitch diagram
on page 150.*

Method

Both the butterflies and the bags come in two sizes: the
smaller size is just right for tiny tots, whereas the second
size will suit bigger people.

Butterflies: There are quite a few little steps to making
the butterflies. Start with a basic body shape, work all the
polka dots and wings as separate pieces and sew them
together bit by bit, then finish off by adding the edging and
antennae. The wings and antennae will naturally curl forwards
somewhat: if you'd like them to lie flatter you can lightly
steam them.

Bags: The gift bags are made in a spiral starting from the
base and working up to the frilly edging, then finished off
by adding little carry handles and decorating with flowers.

Big Butterfly

Wk in spiral TBLs throughout.

Body

With 3.5mm hook and dark pink yarn, mk floop and 1ch.

Rnd 1: 6dc into floop. 6 sts.
Rnd 2: Dc2inc 6 times. 12 sts.
Rnds 3–13: Wk even in dc.
Rnd 14: Wk even in ss.
Fasten off and sew in any loose ends.

Polka dots (make 6)

With 3.5mm hook and dark pink yarn, mk floop and 1ch.
Rnd 1: 6dc into floop. 6 sts.
Rnd 2: (1ss, 1ch) 6 times.
Wk 1ss to join and fasten off. Sew in beg end of yarn on WS and trim close.

Large wing (make 2)

Mk sl-knot and 8ch.
Rnd 1: Sk1ch (this is the t-ch), 6dc, dc3inc in last ch st, rotate piece, 6dc along underside of ch, dc3inc into t-ch from beg of rnd. 18 sts.
Rnd 2: * 6dc, dc2inc 3 times, rep from * once. 24 sts.
Rnd 3: 7dc, dc2inc 4 times, 8dc, dc2inc 4 times. 32 sts.
Rnd 4: 10dc, dc2inc 4 times, 12dc, dc2inc 3 times, 2ss to finish. 39 sts
Fasten off.

Small wing (make 2)

Mk sl-knot and 8ch.
Rnd 1: Sk1ch (this is the t-ch), 6dc, dc3inc in last ch st, rotate piece, 6dc along underside of ch, dc3inc into t-ch from beg of rnd. 18 sts.
Rnd 2: * 6dc, dc2inc 3 times, rep from * once. 24 sts.
Rnd 3: 7dc, dc2inc 4 times, 8dc, dc2inc 3 times, 2ss to finish. 31 sts.
Fasten off.

Finishing

Sew 2 polka dots to each large wing and 1 to each small wing. Sew wings onto body.

Border and antennae

With 3.5mm hook and dark pink yarn and with RS of butterfly facing, wk ch st edging around RH little wing, RH big wing, over head (working 10ch, sk1ch, 9ss then 1ss into body) twice for antennae, then around LH big wing, LH small wing, across lower body, then up again through fabric where body joins RH wings, over head again at base of antennae, then down once more where body joins LH wings. Fasten off. Sew in any loose ends.

Little butterfly

Wk in spiral TBLs throughout.

Body

With 3.5mm hook and light pink yarn, mk floop and 1ch.
Rnd 1: 9dc into floop. 9 sts.
Rnds 2–9: Wk even in dc.
Rnd 10: Wk even in ss.
Fasten off and sew in any loose ends.

Polka dots (make 6)

Wk as for polka dots of big butterfly.

Large wing (make 2)

Wk as for small wing of big butterfly.

Small wing (make 2)

Mk sl-knot and 8ch.

Rnd 1: Sk1ch (this is the t-ch), 6dc, dc3inc in last ch st, now rotate piece and work 6dc along underside of ch, dc3inc into t-ch from beg of rnd. 18 sts.
Rnd 2: * 6dc, dc2inc 3 times, rep from * once. 24 sts.
2ss to finish. Fasten off.

Finishing

Sew 2 polka dots to each large wing and 1 to each small wing. Sew wings onto body.

Border and antennae

With 3.5mm hook and dark pink yarn and with RS of butterfly facing, wk ss edging around RH little wing, RH big wing, then over head, working 1ss, (8ch, sk1ch, 7ss, then 1ss into body) twice for antennae, then around LH big wing, LH small wing, across lower body, then up again through fabric where body joins RH wings, over head again at base of antennae, then down once more where body joins LH wings. Fasten off. Sew in any loose ends.

Bag

Wk in spiral TBLs throughout.
Mk sl-knot and 10[20]ch.
Rnd 1: Sk1ch (this is the t-ch), 1dc, 1htr, 6[16]tr, 6tr in last ch st, rotate piece and wk 8[18]tr along underside of ch, 6tr in t-ch. 28[48] sts.
Rnd 2: * 8[18]tr, (tr2inc) 6 times, rep from * once. 40[60] sts.
Rnds 3–14: Wk even in tr st, ending last rnd with 3htr, 3dc, 4ss.

Frilly edging

Rnd 15: **(1dc, 1htr, 2tr, 1htr, 1dc) in next st, sk 1 st, rep from ** to end. 30 frills.
Rnd 16: Wk one rnd of ss into base of rnd 15.

Handles (make 2)

Mk sl-knot and 46ch.
Sk1ch, 45ss. 45 sts.
1ch, rotate piece and wk 45ss into underside of ch. 90 sts.
1ss in t-ch. Fasten off leaving a tail for sewing.

Flowers (make 3)

With 3.5mm hook and light purple, mk floop and 1ch.
Rnd 1: 5dc into floop. 5 sts.
Rnd 2: Dc2inc 5 times. 10 sts.
1ss to finish. Fasten off.

Finishing

Sew on handles. Sew in any loose ends.

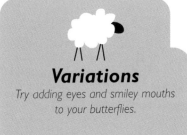

Variations
Try adding eyes and smiley mouths to your butterflies.

Harry the hedgehog has soft 'spikes' and loves to roam among the hedgerows and grasses. You could also try making little shrubs and trees for him to hide under.

Hedgehog

Materials

- Any DK yarn in dark brown, tan and black for hedgehog and green for hedge and grass
- 3.5mm (USE/4, UK9) hook
- 3 small pieces of card for hedge structure
- Darning needle and scissors

Method

Hedgehog: The hedgehog's body is made by starting at the tail and ending at the nose. The yarn is then re-joined at the tail end, and spikes attached (as they are made) to spare front loops around body. An under-body and legs are then added underneath.

Hedge: The zigzag hedge is made of three envelope-style panels, crocheted together on three sides and then stitched together. The hedge is made rigid by pieces of card placed inside the envelope.

Grass: Clumps of grass are formed by working a series of one-row 'blades' and attaching them to a base.

Hedgehog

Work in spiral TBLs throughout body.

Body

With 3.5mm hook and dark brown yarn, mk sl-knot and 15ch, join with ss.
Rnds 1–2: Wk even in ss. 15 sts.
Rnds 3–9: Wk even in dc.

Head

Change to tan yarn.
Rnd 10: (1dc, dc2tog) 5 times. 10 sts.
Rnd 11: Wk even in dc.
Rnd 12: Dc2tog 5 times. 5 sts.
Rnds 13–14: Wk even in ss.
Fasten off and sew in any loose ends.

Spikes

Re-join dark brown yarn to beg of body (at tail end). With 3.5mm hook and dark brown yarn, * wk (6ch, sk1ch, 5ss) to make spike, then surface crochet 2ss into next 2 front loops on body. Rep from * until spikes reach where head begins (Rnd 9).

Underbody and legs

With 3.5mm hook and tan yarn, mk sl-knot and 9ch.
Row 1 Sk1ch, 8dc. 8 sts.
Now wk a rnd of ss edging, working (3ch, sk1ch, 2ss) at each corner for legs. Fasten off, sew underbody to hedgehog and sew in any loose ends.

Finishing

With darning needle and black yarn, sew on eyes and a nose.

Zigzag hedge (make one section in each size)

Hedge section

With 3.5mm hook and green yarn, mk sl-knot and ** 20[22:24]ch.
Row 1: Sk2ch, 18htr. 18 sts.
Rows 2–11[9:7]: 2ch, 18htr.
Fasten off.
Rep from **, but this time don't break off yarn. Put first and second pieces tog (RSs facing outwards) and wk dc edging around three sides.

Finishing

When you have made all three hedge sections (one in each size), sew them tog side by side. Cut card to size so that each size fits into its hedge 'envelope', and place the cards inside for structure.

Grass

Clump of grass (make one or two per base)

With 3.5mm hook and green yarn, mk sl-knot.

Blade 1: 5ch, sk1ch, 4ss.
Blade 2: 7ch, sk1ch, 6ss.
Blade 3: 9ch, sk1ch, 8ss.
Blade 4: 11ch, sk1ch, 10ss.
Blade 5: 9ch, sk1ch, 8ss.
Blade 6: 7ch, sk1ch, 6ss.
Blade 7: 5ch, sk1ch, 4ss.

Fasten off, leaving a 4in (10cm) tail for sewing.

Base

With 3.5mm hook and green yarn, mk sl-knot and 7ch.

Row 1: Sk2ch, 5htr. 5 sts.
Rows 2–5: 2ch, 5htr (work even). Now wk one rnd edging in htr st, working (1htr, 1tr, 1htr) into each corner and finishing with 1dc, 1ss.

Finishing

Sew one or two clumps of grass to each base and sew in any loose ends.

Variations

If you're in a hurry to finish your hedgehog, you could leave off the tan under-body and legs. Alternatively, try using a 'fluffy' or 'hairy' fashion yarn for the body and omitting working the spikes.

The itsy bitsy spider went up the water spout. Down came the rain and washed the spider out. Out came the sun and dried up all the rain, and itsy bitsy spider climbed up the spout again!

Spider

Materials

- Any DK yarn in black, white, red and blue for spider; yellow for sun; white, blue and silver/grey for rain cloud; grey for water spout
- 3.25mm (USD/3, UK10) and 3.5mm hooks (USE/4, UK9)
- Cardboard tube for water spout (a bathroom tissue tube is ideal)
- Darning needle and scissors

For further guidance, see the branching out and turning back stitch diagram on page 149.

Method

Spider: The spider body consists of an inner and outer body, with legs and facial features then added on.

Sun: The sun is made from two centre pieces joined together and rays are then worked outwards in rounds.

Rain: The rain cloud begins much as the sun. Scallops are then added in a spiral by working into 'spare' front loops, and rain is attached as lengths of blue yarn. Finally, a crescent of silver/grey is worked — because, of course, every cloud has a silver lining!

Water spout: Finally, the water spout is created by making two rectangular pieces, joining them on three sides with double crochet and using a cardboard tube for structure.

Spider

Work inner and outer bodies in spiral TBLs throughout.

Inner body

With 3.5mm hook and black yarn, mk floop and 1ch.

Rnd 1: 6dc into floop. 6 sts.
Rnd 2: Dc2inc 6 times. 12 sts.
Rnds 3–7: Wk even in dc.
Rnds 8–10: Wk even in ss.
Rnd 11: (1dc, dc2inc) 6 times. 18 sts.
Rnd 12: (2dc, dc2inc) 6 times. 24 sts.
Wk 2ss to finish. Fasten off.

Outer body

Rnd 1: 6dc into floop. 6 sts.
Rnd 2: Dc2inc 6 times. 12 sts.
Rnd 3: (1dc, dc2inc) 6 times. 18 sts.
Rnd 4: (2dc, dc2inc) 6 times. 24 sts.
Rnds 5–8: Wk even in dc.
Place inner body inside outer body.
Rnd 9: Ss2pcs tog to end. Fasten off.

Legs

Now turn spider body upside down and re-join black yarn to last rnd. Next rnd: * (11ch, sk1ch, 10ss) to mk leg, 3ss into base. Rep from * to end. 8 legs. Fasten off.

Eyes (make 2)

With 3.25mm hook and white yarn, mk floop and 1ch.
Rnd 1: 6dc into floop. 6 sts.
Ss to join, and fasten off. Sew in beg end of yarn to WS of eye. Sew eyes to outer body.

Finishing

Sew in any loose ends. You can steam the legs if you'd like them to be straight rather than curling under.

Sun

Work sun in spiral TBLs throughout.

Centre back

With 3.5mm hook and yellow yarn, mk floop and 1ch.
Rnd 1: 6dc into floop. 6 sts.
Rnd 2: Dc2inc 6 times. 12 sts.
Rnd 3: (1dc, dc2inc) 6 times. 18 sts.
Rnd 4: (2dc, dc2inc) 6 times. 24 sts.
Rnd 5: (3dc, dc2inc) 6 times. 30 sts.
Wk 2ss loosely. Fasten off.

Centre front

Wk as for centre back but do not fasten off.
Put centre front and back tog with RSs facing outwards.
Rnd 6: Ss2pcs tog to last 5 sts, then work rem 5 sts as ss into front centre only (creating finger hole). ***

Rays
Rnd 7: ** (7ch, sk1ch, 1ss, 2dc, 2htr, 1tr, 1j-tr) for ray, then 1ss into next st of centre. Rep from ** to end. 10 rays. The rays will curl over as you make them on this row, but don't worry: this will be corrected by both the next two rows and by steam pressing during finishing.
Rnd 8: Ss around edge of rays, working (1ss, 1ch, 1ss) into each tip.
Rnd 9: Now ss one rnd right through the fabric between the centre and the rays. Fasten off and sew in any loose ends of yarn.

Finishing
To encourage the rays to stay flat, lightly steam (if yarn is acrylic) or steam press (if yarn is a wool or cotton).

Variations
I have designed these puppets to be a little larger than the other sets in this book, on the premise that this playset is more likely to be used by grown-ups to entertain very young children. To make them smaller, try using 4-ply yarn and a smaller hook.

Rain cloud
With 3.5mm hook and white yarn, work as for sun to ***.
Fasten off, then re-join yarn to beg st (at middle of cloud). The 'fluffy' crescent bits of the cloud will be worked in surface crochet, into the spiral of 'spare' front loops. **** Wk (1dc in next loop, 1ch, 3tr in foll loop, 1ch), rep from **** until you've worked to the edge of the cloud. You will now have a nice round cloud: to make this into more of an oval, break off yarn leaving a tail approx 8in (20cm) long and with darning needle run a line of gathering stitches through the centre of the cloud. Fasten off and sew in any loose ends.

Rain
Cut eight pieces of blue yarn, each 6in (15cm) long. Fold each in half and knot onto underside of cloud.

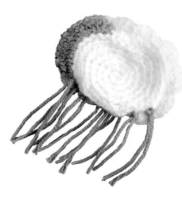

Silver lining
With 3.5mm hook and silver/grey, join yarn to RH side of cloud.
Work 1ch, 1dc, 2tr 6 times, (1htr, 1dc) in next st, and finish with a ss.
Fasten off.

Finishing
Trim rain so that the blue strands of yarn are even lengths. Sew in any loose ends.

Water spout
Inner piece
With 3.5mm hook and grey yarn, mk sl-knot and 27ch.
Row 1: Sk2ch, 25htr. 25 sts.
Row 2 and foll even rows: (RS) Wk even in htr TBL.
Row 3 and foll odd rows: Wk even in fphtr.
Work 21 rows in total.
Fasten off.

Outer piece
Work as for inner piece but do not fasten off.
Place both pieces tog with RS facing you. Dc2pcs tog on three sides, working (1dc, 1ch, 1dc) into corners. Leave fourth side open and fasten off.

Finishing
Cut cardboard tube lengthwise and trim to size if necessary, and place it inside spout 'envelope'. Sew in any loose ends.

Busy bumbly bees buzzing about blithely in the breeze!
Bzzzzz bzzzzz bzzzzz. Pair them up with the ladybug and
butterflies for a woodland party.

Bumble Bee

Materials

- Any DK yarn in black, yellow (or orange) and white for bee, any two bright colours for flower
- 3.5mm (USE/4, UK9) hook
- 2 tiny buttons per bee
- Sewing needle and black thread
- Darning needle and scissors

Method

Bee: These little bumble bee puppets are so easy to make. Stripes are stitched onto a basic body shape, wings are added and then little buttons sewn on for eyes.

Flower: For extra impact, add the colourful over-sized flowers for the bees to land on. They are made with a double-thickness centre and the petals are then added on in a contrast colour.

For further guidance, see the basic body stitch diagram on page 148.

Bee

Work in spiral TBLs throughout body.

Body

With 3.5mm hook and black yarn, mk floop and 1ch.

Rnd 1: 6dc into floop. 6 sts.
Rnd 2: Dc2inc 6 times. 12 sts.
Rnds 3–11: Wk even in dc.
Rnd 12: Wk even in ss.
Fasten off and sew in any loose ends.

Stripes

With darning needle and yellow or orange yarn, make the stripes by overstitching along the spiral for approx 5 rnds.

Wings

With 3.5mm hook and white yarn, mk floop and 1ch.

Rnd 1: (2dc, 2htr, 4tr, 2htr, 2dc) into floop. 12 sts.
Rnd 2: Wk even in ss (loosely) TBLs. Fasten off, leaving a tail for sewing onto the body. Sew in beg end of yarn on WS.

Finishing

With darning needle, sew on the wings. With sewing needle and black thread, sew on tiny buttons for eyes. Sew in any loose ends.

Flower

Work in spiral TBLs throughout centre back and front.

Centre back

With 3.5mm hook and colour 1, mk floop and 1ch.

Rnd 1: 5dc into floop. 5 sts.
Rnd 2: Dc2inc 5 times. 10 sts.
Rnd 3: (1dc, dc2inc) 5 times. 15 sts.
Rnd 4: (2dc, dc2inc) 5 times. 20 sts.
Rnd 5: (3dc, dc2inc) 5 times. 25 sts.
Wk 2ss loosely. Fasten off.

Centre front

Wk as for centre back but do not fasten off.
Put centre front and back tog with RSs facing outwards.
Rnd 6: Ss2pcs tog loosely. Fasten off. Change to colour 2 and wk 1 further rnd in ss (loosely)

Petals

Now wk TFBLs throughout petals.
Row 1: *Work 5dc, turn. 5 sts.
Row 2: 1ch, 5dc (work even).
Row 3: Dc2inc, 3dc, dc2inc. 7 sts.
Rows 4–5: 1ch, 7dc (work even).
Row 6: Dc2inc, 5dc, dc2inc. 9 sts.
Row 7–9: 1ch, 9dc (work even).
Row 10: Dc2tog, 5dc, dc2tog. 7 sts.
Row 11: 1ch, 7dc (work even).
Row 12: Dc2tog, 3dc, dc2tog. 5 sts.
Row 13: Dc2tog, 1dc, dc2tog. 3 sts.
Return to centre side row: (RS) Now dc down left side of petal to get back to the base (1dc into side of each row). *
Work from * to * four more times.
5 petals.
Next rnd: Work all around the edge once, for each petal working 1dc into the side of each row along RH side and into each st at top, then 1ss into each dc down LH side. Fasten off and sew in any loose ends.

Variations

You can use any colours you like for the bees – they don't have to be black and yellow! Pinks and purples, greens and blues... any colours you fancy. Mix and match and use up your stash!

Lions and tigers and bears! Oh my! Leo lion, Tommy tiger and Billy bear are out in the woods today. The basic lion pattern is easily adapted to become either a tiger or bear instead.

Lion and Friends

Materials

- Any DK yarn in tan, brown and white for lion; orange, brown and white for tiger; tan, brown and white for bear
- 3.25mm (USD/3, UK10) and 3.5mm (USE/4, UK9) hooks
- Darning needle and scissors

Method

The basic body pattern is worked as an inner and outer body which are then stitched together after using filling yarn to pad out the head and tummy. The arms and legs are made separately and sewn on, as are the eyes, ears and tail. The nose and mouth are then embroidered. The lion's mane is done in surface crochet. The tiger's stripes are stitched on.

For further guidance, see the outer body and googly eyes stitch diagrams on page 151.

Lion

Work in spiral TBLs throughout inner and outer body.

Inner body

With 3.5mm hook and tan yarn, mk floop and 1ch.

Rnd 1: 6dc into floop. 6 sts.
Rnd 2: Dc2inc 6 times. 12 sts.
Rnds 3–11: Wk even in dc.
Rnd 12: Wk even in ss.
Fasten off.
Cut 2 lengths of yarn: one approx 36in (90cm) and the other 60in (150cm) long. These will be used to stuff the head and body.

Outer body

With 3.5mm hook and tan yarn, mk floop and 1ch.

Rnd 1: 6dc into floop. 6 sts.
Rnd 2: Dc2inc 6 times. 12 sts.
Rnd 3: (1dc, dc2inc) 6 times. 18 sts.
Rnds 4–6: Wk even in dc.
Rnd 7: (1dc, dc2tog) 6 times. 12 sts.
Rnds 8–9: Wk even in ss.
Rnd 10: (1dc, dc2inc) 6 times. 18 sts.
Rnd 11: (2dc, dc2inc) 6 times. 24 sts.
Rnds 12–16: Wk even in dc.
With 3.25mm hook and white yarn, mk floop and 1ch.
Rnd 17: (2dc, dc2tog) 6 times. 18 sts.

Rnd 18: (1dc, dc2tog) 6 times. 12 sts.
Stuff head with 36in (90cm) length of yarn, and wrap the inner body with the 60in (150cm) length of yarn.
Place inner body inside outer body.
Rnd 19: Ss2pcs tog.
Fasten off and sew in any loose ends.

Eyes (make 2)

With 3.25mm hook and white yarn, mk floop and 1ch.
Rnd 1: 6dc into floop. 6 sts.
Ss to join, then fasten off. Sew in beg end of yarn to WS of eye. Satin stitch pupil in brown, tie off and trim ends close.

Mane

With 3.5mm hook, attach brown yarn to lower back of head with a ss.
Wk 5ch, then ss TFL into next stitch.
Cont working (5ch, 1ss) all around the back and top of the head, and under the chin.
Fasten off and sew in any loose ends.

Arms and legs (make 2 of each)

With 3.5mm hook and tan yarn, mk floop and 1ch.
Rnd 1: 6dc into floop. 6 sts.
Rnd 2: (Dc2inc, 2dc) twice. 8 sts.
Rnd 3: Wk even in dc.
Rnd 4: (Dc2tog, 2dc) twice. 6 sts.
Rnd 5: Wk even in dc.
Ss to finish, then fasten off. Sew onto body and sew in loose ends.

Ears (make 2 alike)

With 3.5mm hook and tan yarn, mk floop and 1ch.
Rnd 1: (1dc, 1htr, 2tr, 1htr, 1dc) into floop. 6 sts.
Ss to join, and then fasten off. Sew onto head and sew in loose ends.

Tail

With 3.5mm hook and tan yarn, mk sl-knot..
Wk 15ch, sk1ch, 14dc. Sew tail to lower back and sew in any loose ends.

Finishing

With darning needle and brown yarn, embroider nose and mouth. Sew on eyes using mattress stitch.

Bear

Wk as for the lion, but leaving off the mane and tail.

Variations
The basic lion shape can quite easily be altered to make kitty cats and puppy dogs. Have fun experimenting!

Tiger

Wk as for lion except for the mane, tail and ears.

Ears (make 2)

With 3.5mm hook and white yarn, mk sl-knot.

Rnd 1: Mk3ch, sk1ch, 1ss, 1dc.
Now wk 1 triangular rnd in ss, working 1ch at each of the three corners.
Sew ears onto head.

Tail

With 3.5mm hook and white yarn, mk sl-knot.

Rnd 1: Mk16ch, sk1ch, 15ss.
Sew tail onto body.

Finishing

With darning needle, stitch stripes here and there in brown. For the tail stripes I pulled the yarn tighter at one edge so the tail curls a little.

Lion and Friends

Percy penguin perches playfully on his positively peaceful playground, a nicely icy iceberg, of course. Try making baby penguins too, using 4-ply yarns and smaller hooks.

Penguin

Materials

- Any DK yarn in black, white and red/orange for penguin; white for iceberg
- 3.25mm (USD/3, UK10) and 3.5mm (USE/4, UK9) hooks
- Darning needle and scissors

Method

Penguin: Percy penguin is made from an inner and outer body, each worked from the top downwards and then joined together. The tummy, feet, eyes and beak are made separately and added on.

Iceberg: The iceberg starts out as a basic round-ish piece, working from the centre outwards for the top, then decreasing down again to form the bottom. A wavy edging is then added on.

For further guidance, see the outer body and googly eyes stitch diagrams on page 151.

Penguin

Work in spiral TBLs throughout both inner and outer body pieces.

Inner body

With 3.5mm hook and black yarn, mk floop and 1ch.

Rnd 1: 6dc into floop. 6 sts.
Rnd 2: Dc2inc to end. 12 sts.
Rnds 3–11: Work even in dc.
Rnd 12: Work even in ss.
Rnd 13: (1dc, dc2inc) to end. 18 sts. Finish with 1ss and fasten off.

Outer body

First, set aside about 60in (150cm) of black yarn for stuffing the head later. Then with 3.5mm hook and black yarn, mk floop and 1ch.

Head

Rnd 1: 6dc into floop. 6 sts.
Rnd 2: Dc2inc 6 times. 12 sts.
Rnd 3: (1dc, dc2inc) 6 times. 18 sts.
Rnds 4–6: Wk even in dc.
Rnd 7: (1dc, dc2tog) 6 times. 12 sts.

Neck

Rnds 8–9: Wk even in ss.

Body

Rnd 10: (1dc, dc2inc) 6 times. 18 sts.
Rnds 11–20: Wk even in dc.
Stuff head with the yarn set aside earlier, then place inner body inside outer body.
Rnd 21: Ss2pcs tog to end. Fasten off.

Eyes (make 2)

With 3.25mm hook and white yarn, mk floop and 1ch.
Rnd 1: 6dc into floop. 6 sts.
Ss to join, and fasten off. Sew in beg end of yarn to WS of eye.
Stitch pupils in black, knot ends and trim close. Sew eyes onto face.

Beak

Wk in spiral TBLs throughout.
With 3.25mm hook and red/orange yarn, mk floop and 1ch.
Rnd 1: 4dc into floop. 4 sts.
Rnd 2: (Dc2inc, 1dc) twice. 6 sts.
Rnd 3: (Dc2inc, 2dc) twice. 8 sts.
1ss to finish, then fasten off leaving a tail for sewing.

Feet (make 2)

With 3.5mm hook and red/orange yarn, mk sl-knot and 2ch.
Row 1: Sk1ch, dc3inc. 3 sts.
Row 2: Mk1ch (for t-ch), dc2inc, 1dc, dc2inc. 5 sts.
Edging rnd: Mk1ch, ss along ⅔ of the edge, then on 3rd side wk (1ss, 1ch) 4 times, 1ss.
Fasten off and sew onto lower front edge of body.

Tummy

Wk in spiral TFBLs throughout.
With 3.25mm hook and white yarn,
mk floop and 1ch.

Rnd 1: 6dc into floop. 6 sts.
Rnd 2: Dc2inc 6 times. 12 sts.
Rnd 3: (1dc, dc2inc) 6 times. 18 sts.
Rnd 4: (2dc, dc2inc) 6 times. 24 sts.
2ss to finish, then fasten off.

Wings (make 2)

With 3.5mm hook and black yarn, mk
sl-knot and 10ch.

Rnd 1: Sk1ch (for t-ch), 8dc, (1dc, 1ch,
1dc) in last ch st (to turn corner), 8dc
along underside of ch, (1dc, 1ch, 1dc)
into t-ch.
Rnd 2: * 8dc, dc2inc 3 times, rep from
* once. Wk 2ss to finish, then fasten off.

Finishing

Steam press the beak, flippers and
wings so they lie flat, then sew them
onto your penguin. Finally, sew on the
tummy using mattress stitch.

Iceberg

Wk in spiral TFBLs for rnds 1–11 and
13–22, and TBLs for rnds 12–14.
With 3.25mm hook and white yarn, mk
floop and 1ch.

Rnd 1: 6dc into floop. 6 sts.
Rnd 2: Dc2inc 6 times. 12 sts.
Rnd 3: (1dc, dc2inc) 6 times. 18 sts.
Rnd 4: (2dc, dc2inc) 6 times. 24 sts.
Rnd 5: (3dc, dc2inc) 6 times. 30 sts.
Rnd 6: (4dc, dc2inc) 6 times. 36 sts.
Rnd 7: (5dc, dc2inc) 6 times. 42 sts.
Rnd 8: (6dc, dc2inc) 6 times. 48 sts.
Rnd 9: (7dc, dc2inc) 6 times. 54 sts.
Rnd 10: (8dc, dc2inc) 6 times. 60 sts.
Rnd 11: (9dc, dc2inc) 6 times. 66 sts.
Rnds 12–14: Wk even in dc.
Rnd 13: (9dc, dc2tog) 6 times. 60 sts.
Rnd 14: (8dc, dc2tog) 6 times. 54 sts.
Rnd 15: (7dc, dc2tog) 6 times. 48 sts.
Rnd 16: (6dc, dc2tog) 6 times. 42 sts.
Rnd 17: (5dc, dc2tog) 6 times. 36 sts.
Rnd 18: (4dc, dc2tog) 6 times. 30 sts.
Rnd 19: (3dc, dc2tog) 6 times. 24 sts.
Rnd 20: (2dc, dc2tog) 6 times. 18 sts.
Rnd 21: (1dc, dc2tog) 6 times. 12 sts.
Rnd 22: Dc2tog 6 times. 6 sts.
Fasten off, leaving a tail of yarn for
sewing.
With darning needle, gather the 6 sts
tog and pull tight to close. Fasten off
and sew in any loose ends.

Finishing/edging

Rejoin white yarn to any of the 6
'corners' of rnd 13 and wk TFLs as folls:
Rnd 1: (1ss, 1dc, 1htr, 1tr, tr2inc, 1tr,
tr2inc, 1tr, 1htr, 1dc, 1ss) 6 times. 78 sts.
Rnd 2: (1ss, 1ch) to end.
Fasten off. Sew in any loose edges.

Variations

*Try making a colony of penguins.
You could also make lots of icebergs
stitched together so your
penguins have a great big icy
adventure playground.*

Ferdinand frog sits fretfully on his water lily pad, maybe waiting for a princess to rescue him with a kiss? You could convert him to a red-eyed tree frog by making the legs in yellow and the eyes in red.

Frog

Materials

- Any DK yarn in light green, white and brown for frog and dark green for water lily
- 3.25mm (USD/3, UK10) and 3.5mm (USE/4, UK9) hooks
- Darning needle and scissors

Method

Frog: The inner and outer body are made in a single piece, starting at the inner top, working down, then turning and working upwards (inside out, so the 'wrong side' is used as the right side for a 'bumpy' fabric effect), then decreasing and closing at the top. An eye backing is added, starting with a surface crochet row and then two further rows. Eyes are then made and sewn on. The front and back legs are made and sewn on and then at last a crown is added.

Water lily pad: This starts with a floop, working in rounds and using slip stitches to form the radial notch.

For further guidance, see the frog's legs stitch diagram on page 150 and googly eyes on page 151.

Frog

Work in spiral TFBLs throughout body.

Body

With 3.5mm hook and light green yarn, mk floop and 1ch.

Rnd 1: 6dc into floop. 6 sts.
Rnd 2: Dc2inc 6 times. 12 sts.
Rnds 3–12: Wk even in dc.
Rnd 13: (1dc, dc2inc) 6 times. 18 sts.
Rnd 14: (2dc, dc2inc) 6 times. 24 sts.
Rnds 15–22: Wk even in dc.
Now turn piece inside out so that wrong side is used as RS from Rnd 13.
Rnd 23: (Dc2tog, 8dc, dc2tog) twice. 20 sts.
Rnd 24: (Dc2tog, 6dc, dc2tog) twice. 16 sts.
Rnd 25: (Dc2tog, 4dc, dc2tog) twice. 12 sts.
Rnd 26: (Dc2tog, 8dc, dc2tog) twice. 8 sts.
Rnd 27: Dc2tog 4 times. 4 sts.
Fasten off, leaving a tail for sewing. With darning needle, gather up rem 4 sts to close. Sew in loose ends.

Eye backing

With 3.5mm hook, join light green yarn to the first dc2tog of rnd 24.
Row 1: Mk1ch, then surface crochet 8dc along top. 8 sts.
Row 2: 1ch, 1dc, 1htr, tr3inc, 2htr, tr3inc, 1htr, 1dc. 12 sts.
Row 3: 1ch, 1ss, dc2inc twice, 4ss, dc2inc twice, 1ss. 14 sts.
Fasten off and sew in loose ends.

Eyes (make 2)

With 3.25mm hook and white yarn, mk floop and 1ch.
Rnd 1: 6dc into floop. 6 sts.
With darning needle, stitch pupils in brown yarn. Sew eyes onto eye backing and sew in loose ends.

Front legs (make 2)

With 3.5mm hook and light green yarn, mk sl-knot. Mk6ch, sk2ch, 1htr, 3ss. Fasten off, leaving a tail for sewing and fold into 3 sections. Sew onto body and tuck away loose ends.

Back legs (make 2)

With 3.5mm hook and light green yarn, mk sl-knot.
Mk15ch, sk1ch, 4ss, 5htr, 5tr. Fasten off, leaving a tail for sewing. Fold into three sections. Sew onto body and tuck away loose ends.

Water lily pad

With 3.5mm hook and dark green yarn, mk floop and 1ch.

Rnd 1: 2dc, 2htr, 6tr into floop. 10 sts.

Rnd 2: Tr2inc 10 times. 20 sts.

Rnd 3: Tr2inc 20 times. 40 sts.

Rnd 4: (1tr, tr2inc) 19 times, (mk2ch, 2ss, mk2ch) for radial notch shaping. 59 sts.

Rnd 5: (2tr, tr2inc) to last tr st, mk2ch, ss down radial notch and back up again, mk2ch.

Rnd 6: (3tr, tr2inc) to last tr st, mk2ch, ss down radial notch and back up again, mk2ch.

Rnd 7: (Partial rnd): (3tr, tr2inc) three times, 3tr, 3htr, 3dc, 3ss.

Fasten off and sew in loose ends.

Finishing

Steam press to make flat.

Variations

Why not try making froggie a little crown to wear?

Sammy snail slithers silently, and rather slowly, in search of yummy stuff! I've included a pattern for a leaf as well, to make sure he doesn't go hungry.

Snail

Materials

- Any DK yarn in light blue, red, yellow and dark blue for snail, green for leaf
- 3.25mm (USD/3, UK10) and 3.5mm (USE/4, UK9) hooks
- Darning needle and scissors

For further guidance, see the basic body stitch diagram on page 148.

Method

Snail: The snail body is made first, starting at the head and then working through the body – incorporating a finger hole and then narrowing towards the end. The shell is then made in two halves, stitched together (in slip stitch) just halfway, then stuffed with spare yarn and stitched onto the body. The antennae consist of just an 8-stitch chain each, trimmed closely at the top end and sewn on, and then the eyes are simply stitched on.

Leaf: This starts out as a simple circular piece, with 'leaf-style' shaping beginning on the fourth row. The leaf, when completed, is ironed to make it rather flat and shiny.

Body

Rnds 8–17: Wk even in dc.

Rnd 18: (Mk6ch, sk 6 sts) to make finger hole, 6dc.

Rnd 19: 1dc into each ch st, 6dc.

Rnd 20: (Dc2tog, 4dc) twice. 10 sts.

Rnd 21: (Dc2tog, 3dc) twice. 8 sts.

Rnd 22: (Dc2tog, 2dc) twice. 6 sts.

Rnd 23: (Dc2tog, 1dc) twice. 4 sts.

Fasten off, leaving a tail for sewing. With darning needle, gather rem 4 sts tog to close.

Sew in loose ends.

Shell (make 2 halves, both alike)

Cut a 48in (120cm) length of red yarn for stuffing the shell later.

With 3.5mm hook and red yarn, mk floop and 1ch.

Rnd 1: 6dc into floop. 6 sts.

Rnd 2: Dc2inc 6 times. 12 sts.

Rnd 3: (1dc, dc2inc) 6 times. 18 sts.

Rnd 4: (2dc, dc2inc) 6 times. 24 sts.

Rnd 5: (3dc, dc2inc) 6 times. 30 sts.

Ss2pcs tog halfway around, then fasten off. Stuff the shell with the red yarn set aside earlier, then sew the shell onto the snail body.

Snail

Work in spiral TBLs throughout body and shell.

With 3.5mm hook and light blue yarn, mk floop and 1ch.

Head

Rnd 1: 6dc into floop. 6 sts.

Rnd 2: Dc2inc 6 times. 12 sts.

Rnd 3: (1dc, dc2inc) 6 times. 18 sts.

Rnd 4: Wk even in dc.

Rnd 5: (1dc, dc2tog) 6 times. 12 sts.

Antennae (make 2)

With 3.25mm hook and yellow yarn, mk8ch tightly. Fasten off and sew onto head.

Trim top end of antenna very closely.

Finishing

Sew on eyes in dark blue.

Leaf

Wk in spiral TBLs throughout.

With 3.5mm hook and green yarn, mk floop and 1ch.

Rnd 1: 3dc, 3htr, 4tr into floop. 10 sts.

Rnd 2: (Tr3inc, tr2inc) 5 times. 25 sts.

Rnd 3: Tr2inc 45 times. 60 sts.

Then wk 2htr, 4dc, 2htr, tr2inc, dtr3inc, tr2inc, 2htr, 24dc, (dc2inc, 3dc) 5 times, 7dc.

Now wk 1 rnd of ss, finishing at the 'point' of the leaf.

Turn and wk a ss row through middle of the leaf (as the vein) and then mk15ch, sk1ch, 14ss (for the stem). Fasten off and sew in loose ends.

Variations

Try changing the shaping of the leaf, so that part of it is 'munched'!

Lily the ladybug loves to laze around on leaves on a lovely late autumn afternoon. With her very own leaf to rest on, she is a real ladybug of leisure!

Ladybug

Materials
- Any DK yarn in red, black and white for ladybug; copper brown for leaf
- 3.25mm (USD/3, UK10) and 3.5mm (USE/4, UK9) hooks
- Darning needle and scissors

Method
Ladybug: The ladybug consists of an inner and outer body made separately and stitched together, with legs, polka dots and facial features then added on.

Oak leaf: The leaf is made starting first with the stem and central vein, then building up the outer shape with four partial rounds.

For further guidance, see the googly eyes stitch diagram on page 151.

Ladybug

Work inner and outer bodies in spiral TBLs throughout.

Inner body

With 3.5mm hook and red yarn, mk floop and 1ch.

Rnd 1: 6dc into floop. 6 sts.
Rnd 2: Dc2inc 6 times. 12 sts.
Rnds 3–7: Wk even in dc.
Rnds 8–10: Wk even in ss.
Rnd 11: (1dc, dc2inc) 6 times. 18 sts.
Rnd 12: (2dc, dc2inc) 6 times. 24 sts.
Wk 2ss to finish. Fasten off.
Cut a length of yarn 144in (365cm) long and wrap around inner body as stuffing.

Outer body

Rnd 1: 6dc into floop. 6 sts.
Rnd 2: Dc2inc 6 times. 12 sts.
Rnd 3: (1dc, dc2inc) 6 times. 18 sts.
Rnd 4: (2dc, dc2inc) 6 times. 24 sts.
Rnd 5: (3dc, dc2inc) 6 times. 30 sts.
Rnd 6: (4dc, dc2inc) 6 times. 36 sts.
Rnd 7: Wk even in dc.
Rnd 8: (4dc, dc2tog) 6 times. 30 sts.
Rnd 9: (3dc, dc2tog) 6 times. 24 sts.
Place inner body inside outer body.
Rnd 10: Ss2pcs tog to end.
Fasten off.

Interim finishing

With black yarn, embroider three lines from the centre outwards, to separate the wings and head.

Legs (make 6)

With 3.5mm hook and black yarn, mk sl-knot and 7ch.
Sk1ch, 6ss. Fasten off, leaving a tail for sewing.
Sew onto ladybug body with WS facing upwards (so that the legs curl downwards).

Eyes (make 2)

With 3.25mm hook and white yarn, mk floop and 1ch.
Rnd 1: 6dc into floop. 6 sts.
Ss to join, and fasten off. Sew in beg end of yarn to WS of eye.
With darning needle and black yarn, stitch pupils.

Polka dots (make 6)

With 3.25mm hook and white yarn, mk floop and 1ch.
Rnd 1: 6dc into floop. 6 sts.
Ss to join, and fasten off. Sew in beg end of yarn to WS of eye.

Finishing

Sew on eyes. Sew on the polka dots, and then sew in any loose ends. You can steam the legs if you'd like them to be straight rather than curling under.

Oak leaf

With 3.5mm hook and copper brown yarn, mk sl-knot and 31ch.

Row 1: Sk1ch, 30ss. This forms the stem and central vein.

Now change to partial rounds for making leaf shape, working from one side of the stem, up to the top of the leaf, and down the other side back to the other side of the stem.

Rnd 1: (RS) 6ss (to complete stem), (mk5ch, sk1ch, 2dc, 1htr, 1j-htr), 7ss up along stem, (mk7ch, sk1ch, 3dc, 2htr, 1j-htr), 7ss up along stem, (mk5ch, sk1ch, 2dc, 1htr, 1j-htr), 5ss up along stem, (mk3ch, sk1ch, 1dc, 1j-htr) twice, 5ss down along stem, (mk5ch, sk1ch, 2dc, 1htr, 1j-htr), 7ss down along stem, (mk7ch, sk1ch, 3dc, 2htr, 1j-htr), 7ss down along stem, (mk5ch, sk1ch, 2dc, 1htr, 1j-htr), 1ss into stem. Turn.

Rnd 2: Wk all around in dc, working 3dc into each leaf tip, finish with 1ss into stem. Turn.

Rnd 3: Wk all around in dc, but working (1htr, 2tr, 1htr) into each leaf tip and dc2tog two or three times at vein between each leaf shaping. Turn.

Rnd 3: Wk all around in dc, but working 3dc into each leaf tip and dc2tog twice between at vein between each leaf shaping.
Fasten off.

Finishing

Press lightly to make leaf a bit flatter, or leave curly as is.

Variations

Try making oak leaves in lots of different autumnal colours.

Under the sea

These parrotfish are made in the assorted jewel colours of
a variegated yarn, but could be crocheted in pinks and purples
or any colour you like.

Parrotfish

Materials

- Any DK yarn in variegated colours, plus white and brown
- 3.25mm (USD/3, UK10) and 3.5mm (USE/4, UK9) hooks
- Darning needle and scissors

Method

These little parrotfish are easier to make than they look.
The main part of each fish is worked from face to tail in
a single piece, with fins and eyes added on.

*For further guidance, see the googly eyes stitch diagram
on page 151.*

Parrotfish

Work in spiral TBLs throughout body.

Body

With 3.25mm hook and variegated yarn, mk floop and 1ch.

Rnd 1: 6dc into floop. 6 sts.

Rnd 2: Dc2inc, 1dc, dc2inc twice, 1dc, dc2inc. 10 sts.

Rnd 3: Dc2inc, 3dc, dc2inc twice, 3dc, dc2inc. 14 sts.

Rnd 4: Dc2inc, 5dc, dc2inc twice, 5dc, dc2inc. 18 sts.

Rnd 5: Dc2inc, 7dc, dc2inc twice, 7dc, dc2inc. 22 sts.

Rnds 6–8: Work even in dc.

Rnd 9: Dc2tog, 7dc, dc2tog twice, 7dc, dc2tog. 18 sts.

Rnd 10: Dc2tog, 5dc, dc2tog twice, 5dc, dc2tog. 14 sts.

Rnd 11: Dc2tog, 4dc, dc2tog, 4dc. 12 sts.

Rnd 12: Work even in ss.

Rnd 13: Dc2inc, 4dc, dc2inc twice, 4dc, dc2inc. 16 sts.

Rnd 14: Dc2tog, 6dc, dc2tog twice, 6dc, dc2inc. 20 sts.

Rnd 15: Work even in dc.

Rnd 16: Dc2inc, 8dc, dc2inc twice, 8dc, dc2inc. 24 sts.

Rnd 17: Work even in ss.

Fasten off.

Side fins (make 2)

With 3.25mm hook and variegated yarn, mk sl-knot and 5ch.

Row 1: Sk2ch, 3htr. 3 sts.

Now work a rnd of dc around the edge, working (1dc, 1ch, 1dc) into each corner and finishing with 1ss.

Fasten off.

Top fin

With 3.25mm hook and variegated yarn, mk sl-knot and 7ch.

Row 1: Sk1ch, 6ss. 6 sts.

Row 2: 1ch, turn piece, 6ss along underside of ch, 1ss in t-ch. 6 new sts under chain.

Fasten off.

Eyes

With 3.25mm hook and white yarn, mk floop and 1ch.

Rnd 1: 6dc into floop. 6 sts.
Ss to join, and fasten off. Sew in beg end of yarn to WS of eye.

Finishing

With a darning needle and brown yarn, stitch pupils onto the eyes. Sew eyes on using mattress stitch, and fins using overstitching.

Variations

Try using up odds and ends of yarn by making the different pieces in contrasting colours, rather than using a variegated yarn.

Stella and Stanley the starfish love to lounge on sunny days. They even have their own rocks to relax on. You could use any colours you like to make them, rather than the yellow, orange and blue I have used.

Starfish

Materials
- Any DK yarn in any two bright colours for each starfish, tweedy grey for rocks
- 3.25mm (USD/3, UK10) and 3.5mm (USE/4, UK9) hooks
- Darning needle and scissors

Method
Starfish: Work each starfish from the centre outwards. The smaller starfish is made of a single base with a dotted-line edging (reverse slip stitch) and a finger pocket added on the back. The bigger starfish has a double-sided base which is joined together with a slip stitch edging, leaving a bit of the edge un-joined to create the finger pocket.

Rocks: The rocks start simply as a circle, then are worked straight for a bit, followed by decreases to partially close the piece, and finally stuffed unevenly with small balls of yarn to give a lumpy 'rocky' effect.

For further guidance, see the branching out and turning back stitch diagram on page 149.

Big starfish

Work in spiral TBLs throughout.

Front

With 3.25mm hook and MC yarn, mk floop and 1ch.

Rnd 1: 5dc into floop. 5 sts.
Rnd 2: Dc2inc 5 times. 10 sts. *
Rnd 3: (1dc, dc2inc) 5 times. 15 sts.

Arms

Rnd 4: Wk (11ch, sk1ch, 3ss, 3dc, 3htr, 1tr, 1j-tr, 1dc into base) 5 times.
Rnd 5: Dc up along RH side of each arm, (1dc, 1ch, 1dc) at each tip, ss down along LH side of each arm and ss into each base st. Fasten off.

Back

Work as for front.

Edging

With 3.25mm hook and CC yarn and with RSs of front and back pieces facing outwards, ss loosely all around edge. Fasten off and sew in any loose ends.

Little starfish

Wk as for big starfish to *.

Arms

Rnd 4: Wk (10ch, sk1ch, 3ss, 3dc, 3htr, 1j-htr, 1dc into base) 5 times.
Rnd 5: Dc up along RH side of each arm, (1dc, 1ch, 1dc) at each tip, ss down along LH side of each arm and ss into each base st. Fasten off.

Edging

With 3.25mm hook and CC yarn and with RSs of front and back pieces facing outwards, ss loosely all around edge.
Fasten off and sew in any loose ends.

Finger pocket

With 3.25mm hook and MC yarn, mk floop and 1ch.

Rnd 1: 6dc into floop. 6 sts.
Rnd 2: Dc2inc 6 times. 12 sts.
Rnds 3–7: Wk even in dc.
Rnd 8: Wk even in ss.
Sew finger pocket onto WS of starfish and sew in any loose ends.

Big rock

First, wind some little balls of grey yarn and set these aside (they will be used later as stuffing for the rock).

Work in spiral TFBLs throughout.

With 3.25mm hook and grey yarn, mk floop and 1ch.

Rnd 1: 6dc into floop. 6 sts.
Rnd 2: Dc2inc 6 times. 12 sts.
Rnd 3: (1dc, dc2inc) 6 times. 18 sts.
Rnd 4: (2dc, dc2inc) 6 times. 24 sts.
Rnd 5: (3dc, dc2inc) 6 times. 30 sts.
Rnd 6: (4dc, dc2inc) 6 times. 36 sts. *
Rnd 7: (5dc, dc2inc) 6 times. 42 sts.
Rnd 8: (6dc, dc2inc) 6 times. 48 sts.
Rnd 9: (7dc, dc2inc) 6 times. 54 sts.
Rnd 10: (8dc, dc2inc) 6 times. 60 sts.
Rnd 11: (9dc, dc2inc) 6 times. 66 sts.
Rnds 12–17: Wk even in dc.
Rnd 18: (8dc, dc2tog) 6 times. 60 sts.
Rnd 19: (7dc, dc2tog) 6 times. 54 sts.
Rnd 20: (6dc, dc2tog) 6 times. 48 sts.
Rnd 21: (4dc, dc2tog) 6 times. 36 sts.
Rnd 22: **(3dc, dc2tog) 6 times. 30 sts.
Rnd 23: (2dc, dc2tog) 6 times. 24 sts.
Rnd 24: (1dc, dc2tog) 6 times. 18 sts.

Fasten off, leaving a long tail of yarn for sewing.

Stuff the rock unevenly with the little balls of yarn you wound earlier.

With darning needle, gather the 18 sts tog and pull tight to close. Fasten off and sew in any loose ends.

Little rock

Wk as for big rock to *, then wk even in dc for 5 rnds.

Next rnd: Wk as for big rock from ** to end.

Variations

You could sew little button eyes and smiley mouths onto your starfish. As with all toys for small children, make sure buttons are sewn on firmly.

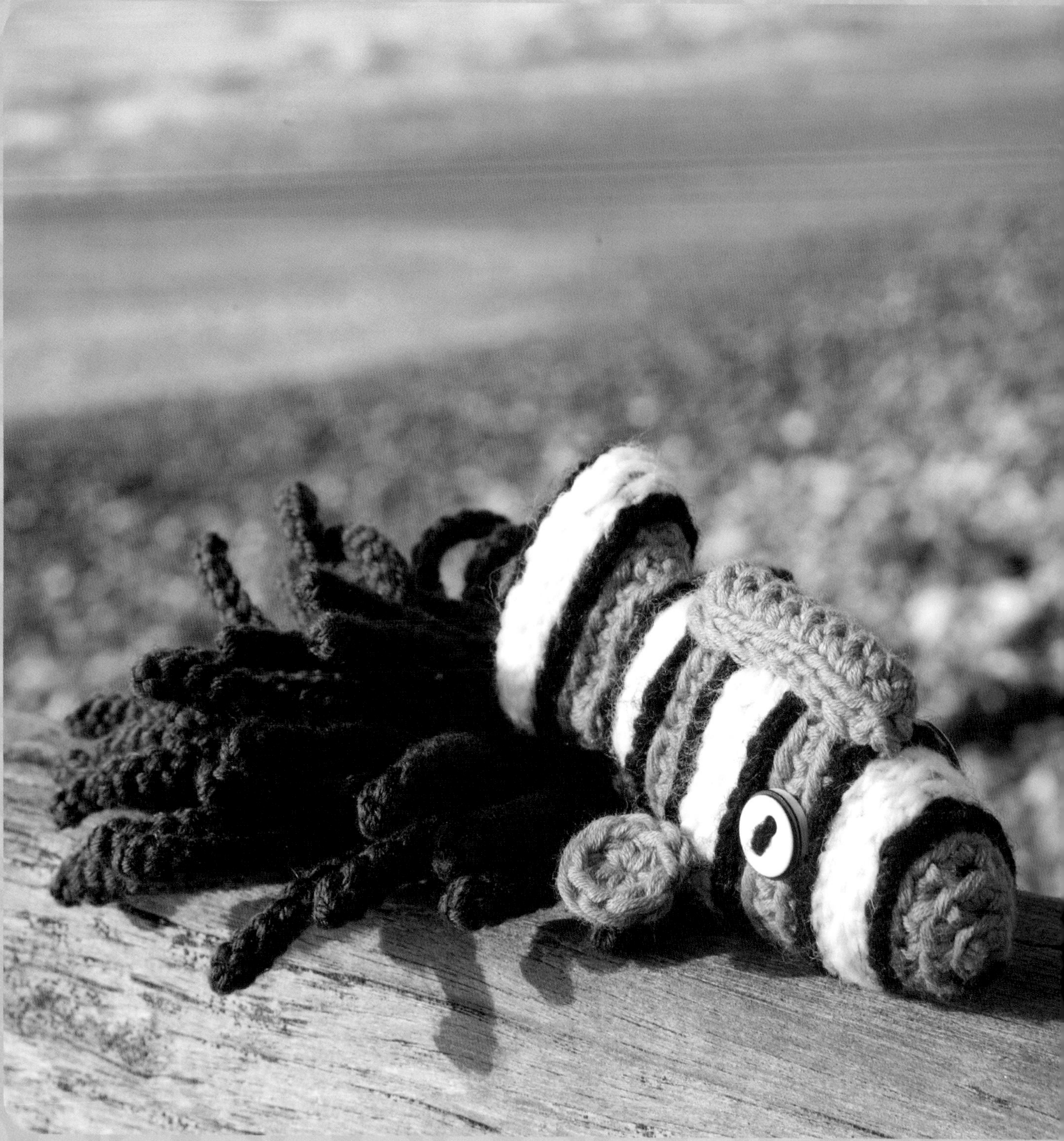

Chuckles the clownfish is a cheeky little chappy, who loves to play hide and seek all day. Why not make him some friends to play with?

Clownfish

Materials

- Any DK yarn in orange, white and black for clownfish; purple for anemone
- Two small buttons for eyes
- 3.25mm (USD/3, UK10) and 3.5mm (USE/4, UK9) hooks
- Darning needle and scissors

Method

Clownfish: The clownfish consists of an inner and outer body, worked separately and then stitched together. The button eyes are then sewn on, and the stripes formed by a combination of surface crochet and overstitching. Finally, the fins are made and sewn on.

Anemone: The anemone is made by working a series of connected chains with a single row of slip stitch each.

Clownfish

Work in spiral TBLs throughout inner and outer body.

Inner body

With 3.5mm hook and orange yarn, mk floop and 1ch.

Rnd 1: 6dc into floop. 6 sts.

Rnd 2: Dc2inc 6 times. 12 sts.

Rnds 3–8: Wk even in dc.

Rnd 9: Wk even in ss.

Fasten off.

Cut a 36in (90cm) length of orange yarn and set aside: you will use this later to stuff the fish between the inner and outer body.

Outer body

With 3.5mm hook and orange yarn, mk floop and 1ch.

Rnd 1: 5dc into floop. 5 sts.

Rnd 2: Dc2inc 5 times. 10 sts.

Rnd 3: (Dc2inc, 3dc, dc2inc) twice. 14 sts.

Rnd 4: (Dc2inc, 5dc, dc2inc) twice. 18 sts.

Rnd 5: (Dc2inc, 7dc, dc2inc) twice. 22 sts.

Rnd 6: (Dc2inc, 9dc, dc2inc) twice. 26 sts.

Rnds 7–9: Wk even in dc.

Rnd 10: (Dc2tog, 7dc, dc2inc) twice. 22 sts.

Rnd 11: (Dc2tog, 5dc, dc2inc) twice. 18 sts.

Rnd 12: (Dc2tog, 3dc, dc2inc) twice. 14 sts.

Place inner body inside outer body and use the 36in (90cm) length of yarn to stuff the space between.

Rnd 13: (Sk 1 st, ss2pcs tog for 6 sts) twice. 12 sts.

Rnd 14: (Dc2inc, 4dc, dc2inc) twice. 16 sts.

Rnd 15: (Dc2inc, 6dc, dc2inc) twice. 20 sts.

Rnd 14: (Dc2inc, 8dc, dc2inc) twice. 24 sts.

Rnd 15: (Dc2inc, 10dc, dc2inc) twice. 28 sts.

Wk 2ss to finish. Fasten off and sew in any loose ends.

Eyes

Sew button eyes into place. Ensure they are sewn on securely if to be given to young children.

Side fins (make 2)

With 3.5mm hook and orange yarn, mk floop and 1ch.
Wk 8htr into floop. 8 sts.
Ss to finish. Fasten off and sew one onto each side of the clownfish.

Top fin

With 3.5mm hook and orange yarn, mk sl-knot and 10ch.
Rnd 1: Sk1ch, 9dc, then rotate work and wk 9dc into underside of ch. 18 sts.
Rnd 2: Wk even in ss.
Fasten off, leaving a tail for sewing.
Fold piece in half lengthwise and sew into place.

Finishing
Stripes

With 3.5mm hook and white yarn, work stripes in ss surface crochet. Fill in if necessary with running stitches using darning needle and more white yarn. Then with black yarn, stitch borders for the white stripes.

Anemone

With 3.5mm hook and purple yarn, mk floop and 1ch.

Base

Rnd 1: 6dc into floop. 6 sts.
Rnd 2: Dc2inc 6 times. 12 sts.
Rnd 3: (1dc, dc2inc) 6 times. 18 sts.
Rnd 4: (2dc, dc2inc) 6 times. 24 sts.
Rnd 5: (3dc, dc2inc) 6 times. 30 sts.
Now fasten off yarn, and rejoin to centremost st TFL.

Tubes

(Mk15ch, sk1ch, 14ss), 1ss TFL of next st in base. Rep from * until you reach the outermost edge of the base.
Fasten off and sew in any loose ends.

Variations

This orange, black and white clownfish may be the best-known variety, but clownfish can come in a number of different colours and stripe patterns. Try black with white stripes and yellow or black fins, rich tomato red with a single white stripe behind the eyes, or maroon with classic white stripes edged with black.

Crabby the crab is actually quite a cheerful fellow, despite his name!
And why not? He's got his very own sandcastle palace, big enough
for him and lots of his seafaring friends.

Crab

Materials

- Any DK yarn in red, white and black for crab; 'sandy' colour for sandcastle bag
- 3.25mm (USD/3, UK10) and 3.5mm (USE/4, UK9) hooks
- Darning needle and scissors

Method

Crab: The crab starts out with an inner and outer body, padded a little with some extra yarn. Eyes on stalks are then added, as are legs and claws.

Sandcastle bag: The gift bag is made in a spiral starting from the base and working up to the castellated edging, then finished off by adding little carry handles and decorating with embroidery for the door and windows.

For further guidance, see the googly eyes stitch diagram on page 151.

Crab

Wk in spiral TBLs throughout inner and outer bodies.

Inner body

With 3.5mm hook and red yarn, mk floop and 1ch.
Rnd 1: 6dc into floop. 6 sts.
Rnd 2: Dc2inc 6 times. 12 sts.
Rnds 3–12: Wk even in dc.
Rnd 13: Wk even in ss.
Fasten off. Cut a length of yarn to 36in (90cm) and set aside for stuffing the body.

Outer body

With 3.5mm hook and red yarn, mk floop and 1ch.
Rnd 1: 6dc into floop. 6 sts.
Rnd 2: (Dc2inc, 1dc, dc2inc) twice. 10 sts.
Rnd 3: (Dc2inc, 3dc, dc2inc) twice. 14 sts.
Rnd 4: (Dc2inc, 5dc, dc2inc) twice. 18 sts.
Rnd 5: (Dc2inc, 7dc, dc2inc) twice. 22 sts.
Rnd 6: (Dc2inc, 9dc, dc2inc) twice. 26 sts.
Rnd 7: (Dc2inc, 11dc, dc2inc) twice. 30 sts.
Rnds 8–11: Wk even in dc.
Rnd 12: (Dc2tog, 11dc, dc2tog) twice. 26 sts.
Rnd 13: (Dc2tog, 9dc, dc2tog) twice. 22 sts.
Rnd 14: (Dc2tog, 7dc, dc2tog) twice. 18 sts.
Rnd 15: (Dc3tog, 3dc, dc3tog) twice. 12 sts.
Place inner body inside outer body and stuff the space between with the 36in (90cm) length of yarn set aside earlier.
Rnd 16: Ss2pcs tog.
Fasten off. Sew in any loose ends.

Eyes on stalks (make 2)

Start with the eye backing.
With 3.5mm hook and red yarn, mk floop and 1ch. Wk 8htr into floop. 8 sts. Join rnd with a ss.

Stalk

(Mk5ch, sk1ch, 4ss), then 1ss into eye backing, then rotate piece and wk4ss into underside of ch.
Fasten off.

Eyeball

With 3.25mm hook and white yarn, mk floop and 1ch.
Rnd 1: 6dc into floop. 6 sts.
Ss to join, and then fasten off. Sew in beg end of yarn to WS of eye. Satin stitch pupil in black, tie off and trim ends close.
Sew eyeballs onto eye backing using mattress stitch and sew in loose ends.
Sew stalks onto body.

Legs (make 2 sets – 1 on each side of body)

Turn Crabby upside down (this is so that the legs curl downwards and not upwards!).

With 3.5mm hook and red yarn, * surface crochet 1ss TFL at side, (mk7ch, sk1ch, 6ss), rep from * 3 times. 1 set (4 legs).

Claws (make 2)

With 3.5mm hook and red yarn, mk sl-knot.

(Mk6ch, sk1ch, 5ss) for first half of claw, (mk6ch, sk1ch, 5ss) for second half of claw, 1ss into very first ss, (mk10ch, sk1ch, 9ss) for arm.

Now wk 1 rnd of ss all around: along underside of arm ch, around first and second halves of claw, then along top of arm again.

Sew on both claws at arm end.

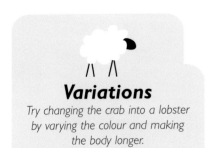

Variations

Try changing the crab into a lobster by varying the colour and making the body longer.

Sandcastle bag

Bag

Wk in spiral TBLs throughout.

With 3.5mm hook and sand-coloured yarn, Mk sl-knot and 20ch.

Rnd 1: Sk1ch (this is the t-ch), 1dc, 1htr, 16tr, 6tr in last ch st, rotate piece and wk 18tr along underside of ch, 6tr in t-ch.

48 sts.

Rnd 2: * 18tr, (tr2inc) 6 times, rep from * once. 60 sts.

Rnds 3–14: Wk even in tr st, ending last rnd with 3htr, 3dc, 4ss.

Castellations

Rnd 15: * (Mk5ch, sk2ch, 2tr, 1 j-tr), 4ss, rep from * to end. 10 castellations.

Rnd 16: * Wk 1 rnd of ss around castellations, working (1ss, 1ch, 1ss) into each upper corner.

Steam press the castellations lightly to encourage them not to curl.

Rnds 17–18: Wk 2 rnds of ss (surface crochet) into base of rnd 15. This is to fortify the top of the bag so the castellations stand up straighter.

Handles (make 2)

Mk sl-knot and 46ch.

Sk1ch, 45ss. 45 sts.

1ch, rotate piece and wk 45ss into underside of ch. 90 sts.

1ss in t-ch. Fasten off leaving a tail for sewing.

Sew on handles.

Finishing

Sew in any loose ends. Embroider the outline for the windows and door.

A warm welcome to Wanda, Wesley and Wilma – the jellyfish trio! Watch them wobble about under the waves together, dancing along the reef and having lots of fun.

Jellyfish

Materials

- Any DK yarn in dark blue for base, any colour for jellyfish
- 3.5mm (USE/4, UK9) hook
- Darning needle and scissors

Method

These little jellyfish are made in one piece from the top downwards. You can make bases for them, so that they stand up on their own when not being played with – or not, as you prefer.

For further guidance, see the branching out and turning out stitch diagram on page 149.

Jellyfish

Work jellyfish in spiral TBLs throughout.

Body

With 3.5mm hook and any colour yarn, mk floop and 1ch.

Rnd 1: 6dc into floop. 6 sts.
Rnd 2: Dc2inc 6 times. 12 sts.
Rnd 3: (1dc, dc2inc) 6 times. 18 sts.
Rnd 4: (2dc, dc2inc) 6 times. 24 sts.
Rnds 5–6: Wk even in dc.
Rnd 7: (2dc, dc2tog) 6 times. 18 sts.
Rnd 8: (1dc, dc2tog) 6 times. 12 sts.
Rnd 9: (1dc, dc2inc) 6 times. 18 sts.

Tentacles

Rnd 10: * 1ss into next st of rnd 9, 12ch, sk1ch, 11ss, 1ss in foll st of rnd 9. Repeat from * 8 times.
9 tentacles.
Fasten off.

Base

Work jellyfish in spiral TBLs throughout. With 3.5mm hook and dark blue yarn, mk floop and 1ch.

Rnd 1: 6dc into floop. 6 sts.
Rnd 2: Dc2inc 6 times. 12 sts.
Rnds 3–9: Wk even in dc.
Rnd 10: (1ss, 1ch) 11 times, 1ss.
Fasten off.

Finishing

Place jellyfish onto base and with darning needle stitch it on so that it stays in place. Sew in any loose ends.

Variations
You might like to add googly eyes and a goofy smile to your jellyfish.

Otto and Olga octopus are obviously obsessed with ogling their beautiful babies Ollie and Olivia. Why stop at two babies? Make another six for a set of octopus octuplets.

Octopus

Materials

- Any DK yarn in any colour for octopus, plus white and blue for eyes and red for mouth
- 3.25mm (USD/3, UK10) hook
- Darning needle and scissors

Method

Each octopus starts at the top of the head, worked downwards in one piece and ending with the tentacles. Eyes are then made and attached, and finally the mouth embroidered.

For further guidance, see the branching out and turning back stitch diagram on page 149 and googly eyes on page 151.

Octopus

Wk in spiral TBLs throughout.

Head

With 3.25mm hook and MC yarn,
mk floop and 1ch.

Rnd 1: 6dc into floop. 6 sts.

Rnd 2: Dc2inc 6 times. 12 sts.

Rnd 3: (1dc, dc2inc) 6 times. 18 sts.

Rnds 4–7: Work even in dc.

Rnd 8: (1dc, dc2tog) 6 times. 12 sts.

Rnds 9–10: Work even in ss.

Rnd 11: (2dc, dc2inc) 6 times. 16 sts.

Arms

Rnd 12: Wk (15ch, sk1ch, 5ss, 5dc,
4htr, 1j-htr, 1dc into base) 8 times.

Rnd 13: Dc up along RH side of each
arm, (1dc, 1ch, 1dc) at each tip, and ss
down along LH side of each arm.
Fasten off and sew in any loose ends.

Eyes (make 2)

With 3.25mm hook and white yarn,
mk floop and 1ch.

Rnd 1: 6dc into floop. 6 sts.
Ss to join, and fasten off. Sew in beg
end of yarn to WS of eye.

Finishing

With a darning needle and dark brown
yarn, stitch pupils onto the eyes.
Sew eyes onto the head using mattress
stitch. Embroider a smiley mouth
with red yarn.

Little octopus

Wk as for big octopus to end of rnd 6.

Rnd 7: (1dc, dc2tog) 6 times. 12 sts.

Rnds 8–9: Work even in ss.

Rnd 10: (2dc, dc2inc) 6 times. 16 sts.

Arms

Rnd 11: Wk (11ch, sk1ch, 5ss, 5dc, 1j-htr, 1dc into base) 8 times.

Rnd 12: Dc up along RH side of each arm, (1dc, 1ch, 1dc) at each tip, and ss down along LH side of each arm. Fasten off and sew in any loose ends.

Variations

You can make your octopodes into squids (with 10 tentacles rather than 8 arms) by increasing to 20 stitches rather than 16 on round 11. Just change the 11th round to: (dc2inc, 1dc, dc2inc) 4 times. 20 sts. Then work the (15ch, sk1ch, 5ss, 5dc, 4htr, 1j-htr, 1dc into base) of the 12th[11th] round ten times rather than eight.

Wanda whale and her baby Wally love whooshing about in the waves!
These two little cuties even have their own little ocean to play in.
You'll have a whale of a time playing with them!

Whales

Materials

- Any DK yarn in light blue, dark blue, white and red for whale; dark blue for ocean
- 3.25mm (USD/3, UK10) and 3.5mm (USE/4, UK9) hooks
- Darning needle and scissors

Method

Both whales are made starting with the inner body and working downwards, then turning back and working upwards for the outer body. The tail, fins and eyes are worked separately and sewn on, then the mouth is embroidered in a single stitch.

For further guidance, see the googly eyes stitch diagram on page 151.

Mamma whale

Work in spiral TBLs throughout.

Inner body

With 3.5mm hook and light blue yarn, mk floop and 1ch.

Rnd 1: 6dc into floop. 6 sts.
Rnd 2: Dc2inc 6 times. 12 sts.
Rnds 3–7: Wk even in dc.
Rnds 8–9: Wk even in ss.

Outer body

Rnd 10: (1dc, dc2inc) 6 times. 18 sts.
Rnd 11: (2dc, dc2inc) 6 times. 24 sts.
Rnds 12–15: Wk even in dc.
Rnd 16: (Dc2tog, 8dc, dc2tog) twice. 20 sts.
Rnd 17: (Dc2tog, 6dc, dc2tog) twice. 16 sts.
Rnd 18: (Dc2tog, 4dc, dc2tog) twice. 12 sts.
Rnd 19: Dc2tog 6 times. 6 sts.
Tuck inner body inside the outer body. Use a little extra yarn as stuffing between the layers if you like.
Fasten off and sew in any loose ends.

Tail fin

Join light blue yarn to tail area and work TFLs of the body.

Rnd 1: 6dc for top of fin, then turn whale over and work 6dc for underside.
Work rest of tail TBLs.
Rnd 2: Wk even in dc.
Rnd 3: (Dc2inc, 4dc, dc2inc) twice.
Rnds 4–5: Wk even in dc.
Close tail
Work TBLs of both top and underside of tail fin to close off.
Rnd 5: Wk 1ch (as t-ch), 1dc, 2htr, 2ss, 2htr, 1dc.
Fasten off and sew in loose ends.

Side fins (make 2)

With 3.25mm hook and light blue yarn, mk floop and 1ch.
Wk 8htr into floop. 8 sts.
Ss to finish. Fasten off and sew one onto each side of the whale.

Spout of water

With 3.25mm hook and dark blue yarn, mk sl-knot.
Mk7ch, sk1ch, 6ss, then mk9ch, sk1ch, 8ss, then mk11ch, sk1ch, 10ss.
Sew onto blowhole of whale.

Eyes (make 2)

With 3.25mm hook and white yarn, mk floop and 1ch.
Rnd 1: 6dc into floop. 6 sts.
Ss to join, and then fasten off. Sew in beg end of yarn to WS of eye. Satin stitch pupil in dark blue, tie off and trim ends close.

Finishing

Sew eyes on and then stitch mouth in red.

Baby whale

Work in spiral TFBLs throughout.

Inner body

With 3.5mm hook and light blue yarn, mk floop and 1ch.

Rnd 1: 6dc into floop. 6 sts.

Rnd 2: Dc2inc 6 times. 12 sts.

Rnds 3-5: Wk even in dc.

Rnds 6–7: Wk even in ss.

Outer body

Rnd 8: (1dc, dc2inc) 6 times. 18 sts.

Rnds 9–11: Wk even in dc.

Rnd 12: (Dc2tog, 5dc, dc2tog) twice. 14 sts.

Rnd 13: (Dc2tog, 3dc, dc2tog) twice. 10 sts.

Rnd 14: (Dc2tog, 1dc, dc2tog) twice. 5 sts.

Tuck inner body inside the outer body. Use a little extra yarn as stuffing between the layers if you like.
Fasten off and sew in any loose ends.

Tail fin

Join light blue yarn to tail area and work TFLs of the body.

Rnd 1: 5dc for top of fin, then turn whale over and work 5dc for underside.
Work rest of tail TBLs.

Rnd 2: Wk even in dc.

Rnd 3: (Dc2inc, 3dc, dc2inc) twice.

Rnd 4: Wk even in dc.

Close tail

Work TBLs of both top and underside of tail fin to close off.

Rnd 5: Wk 1ch (as t-ch), 1dc, 2htr, 1ss, 2htr, 1dc.
Fasten off and sew in loose ends.

Side fins (make 2)

Wk as for Mamma whale.

Spout of water

With 3.25mm hook and dark blue yarn, mk sl-knot.
Mk5ch, sk1ch, 4ss, then mk7ch, sk1ch, 6ss, then mk9ch, sk1ch, 8ss.
Sew onto blowhole of whale.

Eyes (make 2)

Wk as for Mamma whale.

Finishing

Wk as for Mamma whale.

Ocean

With 3.5mm hook and dark blue yarn, mk floop and 1ch.

Rnd 1: (2dc, 2htr, 6tr) into floop. 10 sts.

Rnd 2: Tr3inc 10 times. 30 sts.

Rnd 3: Tr2inc 10 times. 60 sts.

Rnd 4: (1tr, tr2inc) 10 times. 90 sts.

Rnds 5–8: Wk even in tr.

To finish, wk 4htr, 4dc, 4ss. Fasten off and sew in loose ends on WS.

Marianna the mermaid is the princess of the sea, and she has her own pink coral throne. You could sew sequins onto the tail and bodice for extra sparkle.

Mermaid

Materials
- Any DK yarn in blue, tan and brown for mermaid; pink for coral
- 3.5mm (USE/4, UK9) hook
- Darning needle and scissors

Method
Mermaid: The mermaid's tail and bodice are made first in blue. The head and body are made next and the body sewn into the bodice. The arms are made and attached, then the hair is created and sewn on. Finally, the facial features are added.

Coral: The coral throne is made in a single piece as a globe shape which can then be moulded into a 'bean-bag' sort of shape.

Mermaid

Wk TFBLs for edge of tail.

Tail

With 3.5mm hook and blue yarn, mk sl-knot and 10ch.

Row 1: Sk2ch (t-ch), 2tr, 1htr, 3dc, 1htr, 2tr. 9 sts.

Now mk2ch and wk 1ss into base of the last stitch, then rotate piece as next row will be worked along underside of chain.

Row 2: Mk2ch, 2tr, 1htr, 3dc, 1htr, 2tr. 9 sts.

Row 3: Mk2ch, tr2tog, htr2tog, 1dc, htr2tog, tr2tog. 5 sts.

Row 4: Mk1ch, 5dc.

Now change to working in spiral rnds rather than rows.

Rnd 1: (Foundation rnd) Mk1ch, wk 1dc TFL of each of next 5 sts, then turn and wk 1dc TBL of each of those 5 sts. 10 sts. Now wk TBLs for remainder of piece.

Rnd 2: (Dc2inc, 3dc, dc2inc) twice. 14 sts.

Rnds 3–5: Wk even in dc.

Rnd 6: (Dc2inc, 5dc, dc2inc) twice. 18 sts.

Rnds 7–9: Wk even in dc.

Rnd 10: (Dc2inc, 7dc, dc2inc) twice. 22 sts.

Rnds 11–13: Wk even in dc.

Rnd 14: 11dc, mk8ch, sk11 sts (this creates the finger hole at the back of the waist). 19 sts.

Bodice

Rnds 15–17: Wk even in dc.

Rnd 18: 2dc, htr2inc, tr2inc, htr2inc, 1dc, htr2inc, tr2inc, htr2inc, 10dc. 25 sts.

Rnds 19–20: Work even in ss.

Rnds 21: Work one final rnd in ss (right through fabric) at base of rnd 18. Fasten off and sew in any loose ends.

Head

Cut a 48in (120cm) length of tan yarn (for stuffing the head) and set aside. With 3.5mm hook and tan yarn, mk floop and 1ch.

Rnd 1: 6dc into floop. 6 sts.

Rnd 2: Dc2inc 6 times. 12 sts.

Rnd 3: (1dc, dc2inc) 6 times. 18 sts.

Rnds 4–6: Wk even in dc.

Rnd 7: (1dc, dc2tog) 6 times. 12 sts.

Use the length of yarn set aside earlier to stuff the head.

Neck

Rnds 8–9: Wk even in ss.

Body

Rnd 10: (1dc, dc2inc) 6 times. 18 sts.

Rnds 11–16: Wk even in dc.

Fasten off.

Place body inside bodice. With darning needle and blue yarn, sew in place.

Arms (make 2)

With 3.5mm hook and tan yarn, mk floop and 1ch.

Rnd 1: 6dc into floop. 6 sts.

Wk 1ss to join.

The hand is now made. Next you make the arm.

Mk10ch, sk1ch, 9ss, then 1ss into the hand. Turn and wk in ss along underside of ch, finishing with a ss into t-ch.

Fasten off and sew onto body. Sew in any loose ends.

Hair

Wk TBLs throughout hair.

With 3.5mm hook and brown yarn, mk sl-knot and 15ch.

Row 1: Sk1ch, 14dc. 14 sts.

Row 2: Mk1ch, 13dc (leaving final st unworked). 13 sts.

Row 3: Mk2ch, sk1ch, 1dc into second ch st, 13dc. 14 sts.

Rows 4–17: Rep last two rows.

Now rotate piece and gather top of hairdo by working dc8tog along side (gathering the 17 rows tightly tog).

Fringe

Row 1: Mk1ch, then wk dc5inc into the dc8tog st. 5 sts.

Row 2: Mk1ch, 5dc.

Row 3: Mk1ch, dc2inc, 3dc, dc2inc. 7sts.

Fasten off, leaving a tail for sewing. Stitch loosely onto head and sew in any loose ends.

Finishing

With a darning needle and brown yarn, stitch eyes and mouth onto face.

Coral

Wk in spiral TBLs throughout.

Using 3.5mm hook, mk floop and 1ch.

Rnd 1: (2dc, 2htr, 10tr) into floop. 14 sts.

Rnd 2: Tr2inc 14 times. 28 sts.

Rnd 3: (1tr, tr2inc) 14 times. 42 sts.

Rnd 4: (2tr, tr2inc) 14 times. 56 sts.

Rnd 5–9: Wk even in tr st.

Rnd 10: (2tr, tr2tog) 14 times. 42 sts.

Rnd 11: (1tr, tr2tog) 14 times. 28 sts.

Rnd 12: (Tr2tog) 14 times. 14 sts.

Rnd 13: (Tr2tog) 7 times. 7 sts.

Fasten off, leaving a tail for sewing. With darning needle, gather tog rem 7 sts to close. Sew in loose ends.

Variations

Try creating some friends for Marianna by making other mermaids in different colours.

Shawn the shark swims silently and stealthily in the sea... guarding a treasure chest full of silver and gold coins! To retrieve the treasure you'll have to dodge those sharp sharky teeth!

Shark

Materials

- Any DK yarn in grey and black for shark; brown, gold and silver for treasure chest
- 3.5mm (USE/4, UK9) hook
- Darning needle and scissors

For further guidance on making the coins, see the googly eyes stitch diagram on page 151.

Method

Shark: The outer body is made first, working from the nose to the beginning of the tail and stuffing with yarn to fill it out. Then you make the inner body and slip stitch the two pieces together, and afterwards carry on to make the tail. The top fin and side fins are then made and sewn on, followed by embroidery of the eyes, mouth and gills.

Treasure chest: All the main pieces of the treasure chest (i.e. all except the false bottom and coins) are made double-thickness – two pieces made separately and joined together with double crochet. Each of these pieces is edged in gold yarn with a single round of slip stitch, and the chest is assembled using mattress stitch. The false bottom is then made, the chest padded out with spare yarn and the false bottom stitched in. Finally, the coins are made and used to fill the treasure chest.

Shark

Wk in spiral TBLs throughout inner and outer bodies.

Outer body

With 3.5mm hook and grey yarn, mk floop and 1ch.

Rnd 1: 6dc into floop. 6 sts.
Rnd 2: (1dc, dc2inc) 3 times. 9 sts.
Rnd 3: (2dc, dc2inc) 3 times. 12 sts.
Rnd 4: Wk even in dc.
Rnd 5: (3dc, dc2inc) 3 times. 15 sts.
Rnd 6: (4dc, dc2inc) 3 times. 18 sts.
Rnds 7–14: Wk even in dc.
Rnd 15: (4dc, dc2tog) 3 times. 15 sts.
Rnd 16: (3dc, dc2tog) 3 times. 12 sts.
Fasten off. Cut a 96in (245cm) length of yarn and use it to stuff the outer body.

Inner body

With 3.5mm hook and grey yarn, mk floop and 1ch.

Rnd 1: 6dc into floop. 6 sts.
Rnd 2: Dc2inc 6 times. 12 sts.
Rnds 3–7: Wk even in dc.

Join inner and outer bodies

Do not fasten off. Place inner body inside outer body.

Rnd 8: Ss2pcs tog. 12 sts. Do not fasten off. Rnd 9 starts the tail.

Tail

Rnd 9: (Dc3inc, 5dc) twice. 16 sts.
Rnd 10: (1dc, dc3inc, 6dc) twice. 20 sts.
Rnd 11: (2dc, dc3inc, 7dc) twice. 24 sts.
Rnd 12: (3dc, dc3inc, 8dc) twice. 28 sts.
Rnd 13: (4dc, dc3inc, 9dc) twice. 32 sts.
Rnd 14: Wk even in ss (loosely). Fasten off and sew in any loose ends.

Fins (make 3 alike – 1 for top fin and 2 for side fins)

With 3.5mm hook and grey yarn, mk sl-knot and 6ch.

Row 1: Sk1ch, 1ss, 1dc, 1htr, 1tr, 1dtr. 5 sts.
Now wk 1 rnd in dc as edging, working (1dc, 1ch, 1dc) into each of the 3 corners.
Wk 1ss to finish and fasten off, leaving a tail for sewing.
Lightly steam press to make flat.
With darning needle, stitch onto shark body and then sew in any loose ends.

Finishing

With darning needle and black yarn, sew on eyes. Now take another length of black yarn and separate into strands. Using just one strand, stitch on gills and mouth. Tuck away loose ends.

Treasure chest

Wk TFBLs throughout all chest pieces.
Front of chest
With 3.5mm hook and brown yarn, *mk sl-knot and 13 ch.

Row 1: Sk1ch, 12 dc. 12 sts.
Rows 2–8: Mk1ch (as t-ch), 12 dc.
Fasten off.
Rep from * but do not fasten off.
Put both pieces tog and wk 1 rnd of dc2pcs tog, working (1dc, 1ch, 1dc) at each corner.

Back and bottom of chest

Wk as for front.

False bottom

With 3.5mm hook and brown yarn,
mk sl-knot and 13 ch.
Rnd 1: Sk1ch, 12 dc. 12 sts.
Rnds 2–8: Mk1ch (as t-ch), 12 dc.
Fasten off, leaving a tail for sewing.
Fill up the bottom ⅔ of the chest with
spare brown yarn. Then sew in the false
bottom ⅓ of the way down from the
top edge.

Coins (make 20 in gold and 20 in silver)

With 3.5mm hook, mk floop and 1ch.
Rnd 1: 6dc into floop. 6 sts.
Ss to join, and then fasten off.
With darning needle, weave in ends on
WS and trim ends close.

Finishing

Sew in any loose ends, then put the
coins into the treasure chest.

Sides of chest

With 3.5mm hook and brown yarn,
*mk sl-knot and 8 ch.
Row 1: Sk1ch, 7 dc. 7 sts.
Rows 2–8: Mk1ch (as t-ch), 7 dc.
Fasten off.
Rep from * but do not fasten off.
Put both pieces tog and wk 1 rnd of
dc2pcs tog, working (1dc, 1ch, 1dc) at
each corner.
Rep to make second side of chest.

Curved lid

With 3.5mm hook and brown yarn,
*mk sl-knot and 13 ch.
Row 1: Sk1ch, 12 dc. 12 sts.
Rows 2–14: Mk1ch (as t-ch), 12 dc.
Fasten off.
Rep from * but do not fasten off.
Put both pieces tog and wk 1 rnd of
dc2pcs tog, working (1dc, 1ch, 1dc) at
each corner.

Sides of lid

With 3.5mm hook and brown yarn,
*mk sl-knot and 13 ch.
Row 1: Sk1ch, dc2tog 6 times. 6 sts.
Row 2: Mk1ch, dc2tog 3 times. 3 sts.
Row 3: Mk1ch, dc3tog. 1st.
Fasten off.
Rep from * but do not fasten off.
Put both pieces tog and wk 1 rnd of
dc2pcs tog, working (1dc, 1ch, 1dc) at
each corner.
Rep to make second side of lid.

Interim finishing
Edgings

With 3.5mm hook and gold yarn, wk
1 rnd of ss around each of the treasure
chest pieces you have already made,
working (1ss, 1ch, 1ss) into each corner.
Assemble the treasure chest using
mattress stitch and gold yarn. Sew in
all loose ends.

Variations

*Try giving more detail to the
treasure chest by adding a latch
and handles. Also, you could omit
the false bottom of the chest and
fill it with real pennies!*

Tommy and Timmy the sea turtles love tumbling over the tide.
These chilled-out dudes are really into chasing the currents
and surfing the waves.

Turtles

Materials
- Any DK yarn in green and black
- 3.5mm (USE/4, UK9) hook
- Darning needle and scissors

Method
The shell and underbody are made as circles and joined
together with slip stitch (leaving a little space unstitched
for the finger hole). The head, flippers and tail are then
made and sewn on.

Big turtle

Work in spiral TBLs throughout shell, underbody and head.

Underbody

With 3.5mm hook and green yarn, mk floop and 1ch.
Rnd 1: 6dc into floop. 6 sts.
Rnd 2: Dc2inc to end. 12 sts.
Rnd 3: (1dc, dc2inc) to end. 18 sts.
Rnd 4: (2dc, dc2inc) to end. 24 sts.
Rnd 5: (3dc, dc2inc) to end. 30 sts.
Finish with 2ss and fasten off.

Shell

With 3.5mm hook and black yarn, wk as for underbody but do not fasten off.
Rnd 6: Ss2pcs tog until last 5 sts, then wk 5ss along shell only (this creates the finger hole at the tail area). Fasten off.

Head

With 3.5mm hook and green yarn, mk floop and 1ch.
Rnd 1: 6dc into floop. 6 sts.
Rnd 2: (Dc2inc, 2dc) twice. 8 sts.
Rnd 3: Wk even in dc.
Rnd 4: (Dc2tog, 2dc) twice. 6 sts.
1ss to finish, then fasten off.
With darning needle and black yarn, stitch on eyes and mouth, then sew head onto body.

Flippers (make 4)

With 3.5mm hook and green yarn, mk sl-knot and 6ch.
Row 1: Sk1ch, 2ss, 3dc. 5 sts.
Next end: Wk 1 rnd of ss all around, working (1ss, 1ch, 1ss) at each of the three corners.
Fasten off and sew onto body.

Tail

With 3.5mm hook and green yarn, mk sl-knot and 3ch.
Rnd 1: Sk1ch, 2ss.
Fasten off. Sew onto edge of shell above finger hole.

Finishing

With a darning needle, sew in any loose ends.

Variations

You could try making these turtles with dark green rather than black, and changing the flippers into feet – for 'land-based' turtles.

Little turtle

Work in spiral TBLs throughout shell, underbody and head.

Underbody

With 3.5mm hook and green yarn, mk floop and 1ch.

Rnd 1: 6dc into floop. 6 sts.
Rnd 2: Dc2inc to end. 12 sts.
Rnd 3: (1dc, dc2inc) to end. 18 sts.
Finish with 2ss and fasten off.

Shell

With 3.5mm hook and black yarn, wk as for underbody but do not fasten off.
Rnd 4: Ss2pcs tog until last 5 sts, then wk 5ss along shell only (this creates the finger hole at the tail area).
Fasten off.

Head

With 3.5mm hook and green yarn, mk floop and 1ch.

Rnd 1: 6dc into floop. 6 sts.
Rnd 2: Wk even in dc.
Rnd 3: (Dc2tog, 1dc) twice. 4 sts.
1ss to finish, then fasten off.
With darning needle and black yarn, stitch on eyes and mouth, then sew head onto body.

Flippers (make 4)

With 3.5mm hook and green yarn, mk sl-knot and 5ch.

Row 1: Sk1ch, 2ss, 2dc. 4 sts.
Next: Wk 1 rnd of ss all around, working (1ss, 1ch, 1ss) at each of the three corners.
Fasten off and sew onto body.

Tail

With 3.5mm hook and green yarn, mk sl-knot and 2ch.

Rnd 1: Sk1ch, 1ss.
Fasten off. Sew onto edge of shell above finger hole.

Finishing

With a darning needle, sew in any loose ends.

In outer space

Are Martians friendly or fierce? You decide! Your little green people can have happy faces or scary grins and fangs. Try changing the number of arms, eyes and antennaes for a some fun variations.

Martians

Materials

- Any DK yarn in green, white and brown for Martian and red for landscape
- 3.25mm (USD/3, UK10) and 3.5mm (USE/4, UK9) hooks
- Darning needle and scissors

Method

Martian: Each little green man is formed from an inner and outer body which are joined together at the 'foot' round. Antennae, arms and facial features are then added.

Landscape: The red Martian landscape is worked as three separate circles which are then joined and an edging worked around it to finish it off.

For further guidance, see the outer body and googly eyes stitch diagrams on page 151.

Martian

Work in spiral TBLs throughout both inner and outer body pieces.

Inner body

With 3.5mm hook and green yarn, mk floop and 1ch.

Rnd 1: 6dc into floop. 6 sts.
Rnd 2: Dc2inc to end. 12 sts.
Rnds 3–10: Work even in dc.
Rnd 11: Work even in ss.
Rnd 12: (1dc, dc2inc) to end. 18 sts. Finish with 1ss and fasten off.

Outer body

With 3.5mm hook and green yarn, mk floop and 1ch.

Head

Rnd 1: 6dc into floop. 6 sts.
Rnd 2: Dc2inc 6 times. 12 sts.
Rnd 3: (1dc, dc2inc) 6 times. 18 sts.
Rnds 4–6: Wk even in dc.

Neck

Rnds 7-9: Wk even in ss.

Body

Rnds 10–15: Wk even in dc.

Feet

Place inner body inside outer body. As you work the next rnd you will ss2pcs tog to join the inner and outer bodies.

Rnd 16: * 3ss, (1dc, 1htr, 2tr, 1htr, 1dc) into next st, rep from * once, ss to end. 28 sts.
Rnd 17: Wk even in ss.
Fasten off.

Antenna (make 1, 2 or 3 per Martian)

With 3.5mm hook and green yarn, mk sl-knot and 7ch.
Sk1ch, 3dc in next ch, dc to end.
Fasten off.

Arms (make 2 per Martian)

With 3.5mm hook and green yarn, mk sl-knot and 7ch.
Sk2ch, (3tr in next ch, mk2ch, 1ss in same ch as 3tr) for hand, 3ss for arm. Mk1ch, then ss once all around the edge of piece.
Fasten off.

Eyes (make 2 per Martian)

With 3.25mm hook and white yarn, mk floop and 1ch.
Rnd 1: 6dc into floop. 6 sts.
Ss to join, and fasten off. Sew in beg end of yarn to WS of eye.

Finishing

With a darning needle and dark brown yarn, stitch pupils onto the eyes and a nose and mouth onto the face. Sew eyes onto the face using mattress stitch. Sew antennae and arms onto body.

Finishing

Join pods tog using mattress stitch.

Edging

Wk TBLs throughout edging.
Rejoin red yarn to any point along
3-circle piece, mk2ch, (2tr, tr2inc) all
around edge of 3-circle piece to end,
ss to 1st tr st to finish.
Fasten off. Sew in any loose edges.

Variations

*Your Martian landscape can double
as a teleportation device.*

Martian landscape

Work pods in spiral TFBLs.

Pods (make 3)

Using 3.5mm hook and red yarn, mk
floop and 1ch.
Rnd 1: (1dc, 1htr, 10tr) into floop.
12 sts.
Rnd 2: Tr2inc 12 times. 24 sts.
Rnd 3: (1tr, tr2inc) 12 times. 36 sts.
Rnd 4: (1tr, tr2inc) 16 times. 48 sts.
Fasten off, leaving an 8in (20cm) tail.

Crocheted Finger Puppets

Allie and Annie are amicable aliens from the planet Abboo-dabboo, and are the guardians of the Black Hole of Doom – which conveniently doubles as a gift bag, handy for tidying up your toys.

Aliens

Materials

- Any DK yarn in grey and black for alien; black, grey and yellow for black hole bag
- 3.5mm (USE/4, UK9) hook
- Darning needle and scissors

Method

Alien: Each alien is worked from the top of the head downwards, making the arms and legs as you go. Eyes are worked separately and sewn on, then the mouth is embroidered.

Black hole bag: The bag is made in one piece starting at the pointy end, working upwards to the opening and finishing with a chain stitch handle. Stars and swirls can then be added for decoration.

For further guidance, see the outer body and googly eyes stitch diagrams on page 151.

Alien

Work in spiral TBLs throughout body.

Head

With 3.5mm hook and grey yarn, mk floop and 1ch.

Rnd 1: 6dc into floop. 6 sts.

Rnd 2: Dc2inc 6 times. 12 sts.

Rnd 3: (1dc, dc2inc) 6 times. 18 sts.

Rnd 4: (2dc, dc2inc) 6 times. 24 sts.

Rnds 5–8: Work even in dc.

Rnd 9: (2dc, dc2tog) 6 times. 18 sts.

Rnd 10: (1dc, dc2tog) 6 times. 12 sts.

Rnds 11–15: Work even in dc.

Arms

Rnd 16: * Wk (15ch, sk3ch, tr5inc, 11ss) for arm, 6dc, rep from * once.

Rnds 17–21: Wk even in dc.

Now wk 2 more stitches in dc. This is because when working in spiral rnds, the sts tend to 'drift' a little to the right. By working these 2 extra stitches the legs will line up with the arms better.

Legs

Rnd 22: Wk (15ch, sk3ch, tr5inc, 11ss) for first leg, 6dc, (15ch, sk1ch, tr5inc, 11ss) for second leg, 6ss to finish. Fasten off and sew in any loose ends.

Eyes (make 2)

With 3.5mm hook and grey yarn, mk floop and 1ch.

Rnd 1: 8htr into floop. 8 sts. Ss to join, and fasten off. Sew in ends on WS.

Rnd 2: Join black yarn and wk 1 rnd in ss (loosely).

Fasten off, leaving a tail for stitching the pupils and sewing eyes onto head.

Finishing

With a darning needle, stitch pupils onto the eyes, then sew eyes onto the head using mattress stitch.

Embroider a mouth with black yarn.

Black hole bag

Wk in spiral TBLs throughout.

With 3.5mm hook and black yarn, mk floop and 1ch.

Rnd 1: 2dc, 2htr, 2tr into floop. 6 sts.

Rnd 2: Tr2inc 6 times. 12 sts.

Rnds 3, 5, 7, 9, and 11: Wk even in tr.

Rnd 4: (1tr, tr2inc) 6 times. 18 sts.

Rnd 6: (2tr, tr2inc) 6 times. 24 sts.

Rnd 8: (3tr, tr2inc) 6 times. 30 sts.

Rnd 10: (4tr, tr2inc) 6 times. 36 sts.

Rnd 12: (5tr, tr2inc) 6 times. 42 sts.

Rnd 13: (6tr, tr2inc) 6 times. 48 sts.

Rnd 14: (7tr, tr2inc) 6 times. 54 sts.

Rnd 15: (8tr, tr2inc) 6 times. 60 sts.

Rnd 16: (9tr, tr2inc) 6 times. 66 sts.

Rnd 17: (10tr, tr2inc) 6 times. 72 sts.

Rnd 18: (11tr, tr2inc) 6 times. 78 sts.

Rnds 19–20: Wk even in tr.

Now wk 4htr, 4dc, 4ss to finish smoothly.

Handle

Wk 60 ch sts, skip 39 sts, 1ss to attach handle.

Fasten off and sew in loose ends.

Finishing

Embroider stars and swirls in silvery grey and golden yellow.

Variations

Try embroidering planets onto the black hole, and changing the grey and black of the aliens to bright funky colours.

Rusty and Shiny are renegade robots who are ridiculously resolute about rebelling against... well, everything! You could make a whole army of robots, working for the villain 'Emperor Badguy' (see page 133).

Robots

Materials
- Any DK yarn in silver or gold as MC, plus white and black for eyes and mouth
- 3.25mm (USD/3, UK10) and 3.5mm (USE/4, UK9) hooks
- Darning needle and scissors

Method
The robot consists of an inner and outer body, worked separately and then stitched together. The antenna, arms and facial features are then made and added on.

For further guidance, see the outer body stitch diagram on page 151.

Robot

Work in spiral TFBLs throughout inner and outer body.

Inner body

With 3.5mm hook and MC yarn, mk floop and 1ch.

Rnd 1: 6dc into floop. 6 sts.
Rnd 2: Dc2inc 6 times. 12 sts.
Rnds 3–8: Wk even in dc.
Rnd 9: Wk even in ss.
Rnd 10: (1dc, dc2inc) 6 times. 18 sts.
Rnd 11: (2dc, dc2inc) 6 times. 24 sts.
Fasten off.

Outer body

With 3.5mm hook and MC yarn, mk floop and 1ch.

Rnd 1: 6dc into floop. 6 sts.
Rnd 2: Dc2inc 6 times. 12 sts.
Rnds 3–5: Wk even in dc.
Rnd 6: (1dc, dc2inc) 6 times. 18 sts.
Rnds 7–9: Wk even in dc.
Rnd 10: (2dc, dc2inc) 6 times. 24 sts.
Rnds 11–13: Wk even in dc.
Place inner body inside outer body.
Rnd 14: Ss2pcs tog.
Fasten off and sew in any loose ends.

Arms (make 2)

With 3.25mm hook and MC yarn, mk sl-knot and 10ch.
Rnd 1: Ss all around once.

Hand

(Mk4ch, sk1ch, 3ss) twice, ss into end of arm to secure hand. Fasten off and sew arms onto the sides of the robot's body.

Eyes

With 3.25mm hook and white yarn, mk sl-knot and 4ch.

Rnd 1: Sk1ch, 2dc, dc2inc, rotate piece and wk 2dc, dc2inc into underside of ch. 8 sts.

Rnd 2: Wk even in ss (loosely). Fasten off. With darning needle, satin stitch the pupils in black. Sew the eyepiece in place onto the robot's face.

Antenna (make 1 or more per robot)
Stem

With 3.25mm hook and MC yarn, mk sl-knot and 5ch. Ss all around once.

Top bit

Row 1: 2dc into end of stem.

Rows 2–3: 1ch (as t-ch), 2dc (wkg even in dc).

Now change to working round rather than rows. Wk 1 rnd in ss (loosely) around top bit

Fasten off. With darning needle, sew onto top of head.

Finishing

With darning needle and black yarn, sew on mouth using dotted-line stitch.

Variations

Try making robots in mix-and-match bright colours, with different numbers of antennae, arms and eyes.

Meet the Supernova Ninjas, super-cool defenders of the universe. They are an elite squad of martial arts experts, coming soon to a galaxy near you...

Ninjas

Materials

- Any DK yarn in tan (or other skin-tone colour) for head, a contrast colour for facial features and any colour for cloak
- 3.25mm (USD/3, UK10) and 3.5mm (USE/4, UK9) hooks
- Darning needle and scissors

Method

Make your ninja's head first, and embroider the facial features. The cloak is then made in one piece from the hood down, working over the head and attaching it as you go.

For further guidance, see the hooded cloak stitch diagram on page 152.

Hood

With 3.5mm hook and MC yarn, mk floop and 1ch.

Rnd 1: 6dc into floop. 6 sts.

Rnd 2: Dc2inc 6 times. 12 sts.

Rnd 3: (1dc, dc2inc) 6 times. 18 sts.

Rnds 4–6: 9ss (shaping hood above face), 9dc.

Rnd 7: 9ch (closing the hood under chin), sk 9 sts, 9ss.

Rnds 8–9: Wk even in ss.

Now put head inside hood and stitch into place.

Ninja

Work in spiral TFBLs throughout head.

Head

With 3.25mm hook and tan yarn, mk floop and 1ch.

Rnd 1: 6dc into floop. 6 sts.

Rnd 2: Dc2inc 6 times. 12 sts.

Rnds 3–6: Wk even in dc.

Rnd 7: Wk even in ss.

Fasten off. Embroider facial features and set aside.

Cloak

Work in spiral TBLs throughout cloak.

Shoulders

Rnd 10: (Dc2inc, 8dc) twice. 20 sts.

Rnds 11–12: Work even in dc.

Cuffs rnd

Rnd 13: * Dc2inc twice, 8dc, rep from
* once. 24 sts.

End cuffs

Rnd 14: (Sk5, 7dc) twice. 14 sts.

Rnds 15–16: Work even in dc.

Rnd 17: Dc2inc 14 times. 28 sts.

Rnd 18: Wk even in ss.

Fasten off and sew in any loose ends.

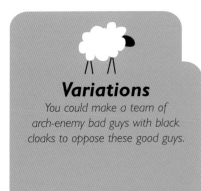

Variations

*You could make a team of
arch-enemy bad guys with black
cloaks to oppose these good guys.*

Superfred the shape-shifter is the hero of the Universe, fighting evil with help from his team of supernova ninjas. He has the ability to shift into 'Lightning Lad', 'Water Wonder' or 'Tornado Triumph'.

Hero

Materials

- Any DK yarn in tan, blue and black for hero; red and yellow for Lightning Lad outfit; light blue and medium blue for Water Wonder outfit; brown and tan for Tornado Triumph outfit
- 3.5mm (USE/4, UK9) hook
- Darning needle and scissors

For further guidance, see the outer body stitch diagram on page 151.

Method

Hero: Our superhero is wearing a blue jumpsuit, so there are colour changes between tan and blue in the outer body and the limbs. There is an inner body as well as an outer head/body, which are made separately and then slip-stitched together. The arms and legs are made then and sewn on. Finally, the facial features are embroidered and spiky hair added on.

Outfits: Superfred's shape-shifting abilities mean that he has three outfits to choose from. Each is formed from a circular piece at the front and a cape-shaped piece at the back. These are then edged in slip stitch and joined with chain stitch along the way.

Hero

Work in spiral TBLs throughout both inner and outer body pieces.

Inner body

With 3.5mm hook and blue yarn, mk floop and 1ch.

Rnd 1: 6dc into floop. 6 sts.
Rnd 2: Dc2inc to end. 12 sts.
Rnds 3–9: Work even in dc.
Rnd 10: Work even in ss.
Fasten off.

Cut a 60in (150cm) length of blue yarn and wrap it loosely around inner body as stuffing.

Outer body

Cut a 48in (120cm) length of tan yarn (for stuffing the head) and set aside.

Head

With 3.5mm hook and tan yarn, mk floop and 1ch.

Rnd 1: 6dc into floop. 6 sts.
Rnd 2: Dc2inc 6 times. 12 sts.
Rnd 3: (1dc, dc2inc) 6 times. 18 sts.
Rnds 4–6: Wk even in dc.
Rnd 7: (1dc, dc2tog) 6 times. 12 sts.
Use the length of tan yarn set aside earlier to stuff the head.

Neck

Rnds 8–9: Wk even in ss.

Body

Now change to blue yarn.

Rnd 10: Wk even in ss.
Rnd 11: (1dc, dc2inc) 6 times. 18 sts.
Rnds 12–19: Wk even in dc.
Rnd 20: (2ss, sk1 st) 6 times. 12 sts.
Place inner body inside outer body.
Rnd 21: Ss2pcs tog.
Fasten off and sew in loose ends.

Arms (make 2)

With 3.5mm hook and tan yarn, mk floop and 1ch.

Rnd 1: 6dc into floop. 6 sts.
Rnd 2: (1ss, mk1ch) 6 times. 12 sts.
The hand is now made. Next you change to blue yarn to make the arm. Wk 1ss, mk7ch, sk1ch, 6ss, then 1ss into the hand. Turn and wk in ss along underside of ch, finishing with a ss into t-ch.
Fasten off and sew onto body. Sew in any loose ends.

Legs (make 2)

With 3.5mm hook and tan yarn, mk floop and 1ch.

Rnd 1: 6dc into floop. 6 sts.
Rnd 2: (1ss, mk1ch) 6 times. 12 sts.
The foot is now made. Change to blue yarn to make the leg.
1ss, mk10ch, sk1ch, 9ss, then 1ss into the foot. Turn and wk in ss along underside of ch, finishing with a ss into t-ch.
Fasten off and sew onto body. Sew in any loose ends.

Finishing

Face

With darning needle and black yarn, sew eyes and mouth.

Hair

With 3.5mm hook and black yarn, mk spikey hair by working (1ss TFL into head, 3ch, sk1ch, 2ss) until you are happy that your superhero has enough hair. Steam press the hair to straighten it, if you like.

Outfits

Work front in spiral TBLs. Wk in red for Lightning Lad, light blue for Water Wonder and brown for Tornado Triumph.

Front

Using 3.5mm hook, mk floop and 1ch.

Rnd 1: (2dc, 2htr, 10tr) into floop. 14 sts.

Rnd 2: Tr2inc 14 times. 28 sts.

Rnd 3: (1tr, tr2inc) 14 times. 42 sts. Wk (2htr, 2dc, 2ss) to finish, then fasten off.

Back

Work back in rows TFBLs.

Using 3.5mm hook, mk sl-knot and 20ch.

Row 1: Sk2ch (t-ch), 6tr, 6htr, 6dc. 18 sts.

Rows 2, 4 and 6: Mk1ch (t-ch), 6dc, 6htr, 6tr.

Rows 3, 5 and 7: Mk2ch (t-ch), 6tr, 6htr, 6dc.

Do not fasten off.

Shoulder straps and edging

Mk2ch (LH shoulder strap), join with ss to front of outfit and wk in ss around until 5 sts before end of rnd, mk2ch (RH shoulder strap), then join with ss to other side of cape and wk in ss around 3 sides of back, working (1ss, 1ch, 1ss) into both bottom corners. Fasten off and sew in loose ends. To dress the hero in his shape-shifter disguise, just slip the outfit over his head.

Finishing

Lightning Lad

With darning needle and yellow yarn, embroider 'LL' onto front and back of outfit.

Water Wonder

With darning needle and medium blue yarn, embroider 'WW' onto front and back of outfit.

Tornado Triumph

With darning needle and tan yarn, embroider 'TT' onto front and back of outfit.

Variations

How about giving Superfred other superpowers, by making him additional outfits? You could also make him a team of supernova ninjas from the ninja pattern in this book.

Watch out for these small but mighty monsters – they make magical mischievous mayhem wherever they go! They would make awesome minions for Emperor Badguy.

Monsters

Materials

- Any DK yarn in green, yellow, light blue, dark blue, red and white.
- 3.5mm (USE/4, UK9) hook
- Darning needle and scissors

Method

The inner and outer body are made in a single piece, starting at the inner top, working down, then turning and working upwards (inside out, so the wrong side is used as the right side for a 'bumpy' fabric effect) then decreasing and closing at the top. Curly-wurlies are added to the top of the head, legs added at the base of the body, then eyes and a mouth.

Monster

Work in spiral TFBLs throughout body.

Body

With 3.5mm hook and green yarn, mk floop and 1ch.

Rnd 1: 6dc into floop. 6 sts.

Rnd 2: Dc2inc 6 times. 12 sts.

Rnds 3–8: Wk even in dc.

Rnds 9–10: Wk even in ss.

Rnd 11: (1dc, dc2inc) 6 times. 18 sts.

Rnds 12–17: Wk even in dc.

Now turn piece inside out from rnd 11, so that wrong side is used as RS.

Rnd 18: (1dc, dc2tog) 6 times. 12 sts.

Rnd 19: Dc2tog 6 times. 6 sts.

Fasten off, leaving a tail for sewing. With darning needle, gather up rem sts to close. Sew in loose ends.

Curly-wurlies

With 3.5mm hook and yellow yarn, mk sl-knot.

*Mk21ch, (sk2ch, 1ss into 3rd ch st) 7 times, rep from * twice. 3 curly-wurlies. Fasten off, leaving a tail for sewing. Sew onto top of head and tuck away loose ends.

Legs (make 4)

With 3.5mm hook and light blue yarn, mk sl-knot.

Mk15ch, sk3ch, tr5inc, 11ss. Fasten off, leaving a tail for sewing. Sew onto base of body and tuck away loose ends.

Eyes (make 2)

With 3.5mm hook and orange yarn, mk floop and 1ch.

Rnd 1: 6dc into floop. 6 sts.

Rnd 2: Wk even in ss (loosely).

With darning needle, stitch pupils in dark blue yarn. Sew eyes onto face using mattress stitch and work 3 rnds of a running stitch around each eye to build up the colour. Sew in loose ends.

Variations

Try making a platoon of these in stark black and white and red, for extra scary-ness.

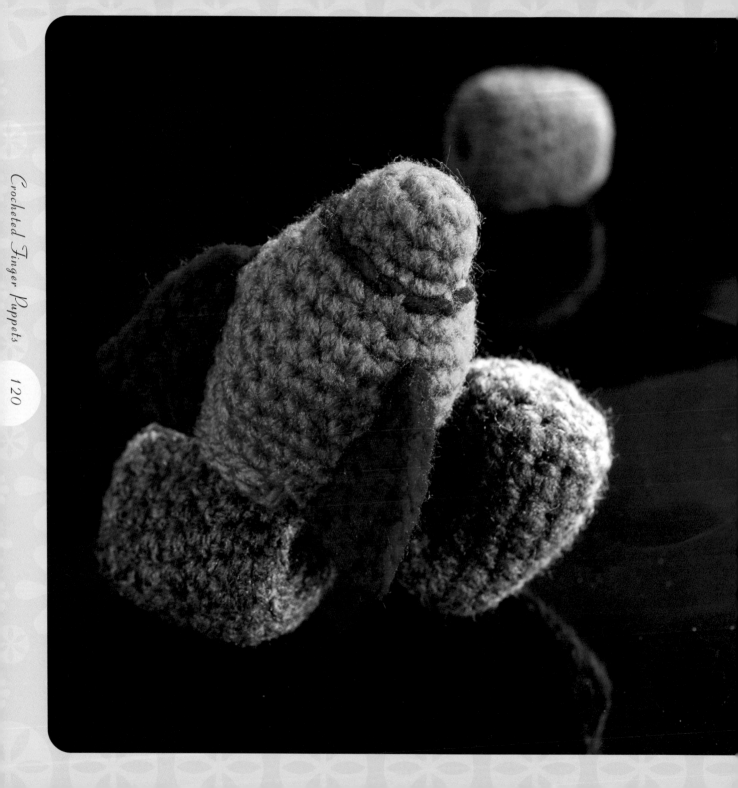

Zoom around the galaxy with this supersonic rocket... but watch out for the meteor storm! The meteors can also be worked in red, to make them 'red-hot'.

Rocket

Materials

- Any DK yarn in blue and red for rocket; dark grey for meteors
- 3.5mm (USE/4, UK9) hook
- Darning needle and scissors

Method

Rocket: The inner and outer pieces are made separately and then slip-stitched together. The fins are then made and sewn on.

Meteors: The inner and outer are bits are made in a single piece, starting at the inner top, working down, then turning and working upwards (inside out, so the 'wrong side' is used as the right side for a 'bumpy' fabric effect) then decreasing and closing at the top.

Rocket

Work in spiral TFBLs throughout.

Inner piece

With 3.5mm hook and blue yarn, mk floop and 1ch.

Rnd 1: 6dc into floop. 6 sts.
Rnd 2: Dc2inc 6 times. 12 sts.
Rnds 3–8: Wk even in dc.
Rnds 9–10: Wk even in ss.
Rnd 11: (1dc, dc2inc) 6 times. 18 sts.
Fasten off. Cut a 36in (90cm) length of blue yarn and wrap around inner piece as stuffing.

Outer piece

With 3.5mm hook and blue yarn, mk floop and 1ch.

Rnd 1: 6dc into floop. 6 sts.
Rnd 2: Dc2inc 6 times. 12 sts.
Rnds 3–4: Wk even in dc.
Rnd 5: (1dc, dc2inc) 6 times. 18 sts.
Rnds 6: Wk even in dc.
Rnd 7: (2dc, dc2inc) 6 times. 24 sts.
Rnds 8–9: Wk even in dc.
Rnd 10: (2dc, dc2tog) 6 times. 18 sts.
Rnd 11–13: Wk even in dc.
Place inner piece inside outer piece.
Rnd 14: Ss2pcs tog.
Fasten off and sew in any loose ends.

Fins (make 3 alike)

With 3.5mm hook and red yarn, mk sl-knot and 7ch.

Row 1: Sk1ch, 1ss, 2dc, 2htr, 1tr.
Next row: Wk 1 rnd in ss, working (1ss, 1ch, 1ss) into each corner.
Fasten off and sew onto base of rocket.

Finishing

With darning needle and red yarn, stitch around the rocket along rnd 5 (to define the nose cone). Sew in any loose ends.

Meteors

Work in spiral TFBLs throughout.
With 3.5mm hook and dark grey yarn,
mk floop and 1ch.

Rnd 1: 6dc into floop. 6 sts.

Rnd 2: Dc2inc 6 times. 12 sts.

Rnds 3–8: Wk even in dc.

Rnds 9–10: Wk even in ss.

Rnd 11: (1dc, dc2inc) 6 times. 18 sts.

Rnds 12–17: Wk even in dc.

Now turn piece inside out so that
'wrong side' is used as RS.

Rnd 18: (1dc, dc2tog) 6 times. 12 sts.

Rnd 19: Dc2tog 6 times. 6 sts.

Fasten off, leaving a tail for sewing.
With darning needle, gather up rem sts
to close. Sew in loose ends.

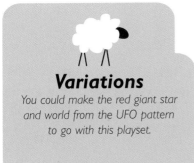

Variations

You could make the red giant star
and world from the UFO pattern
to go with this playset.

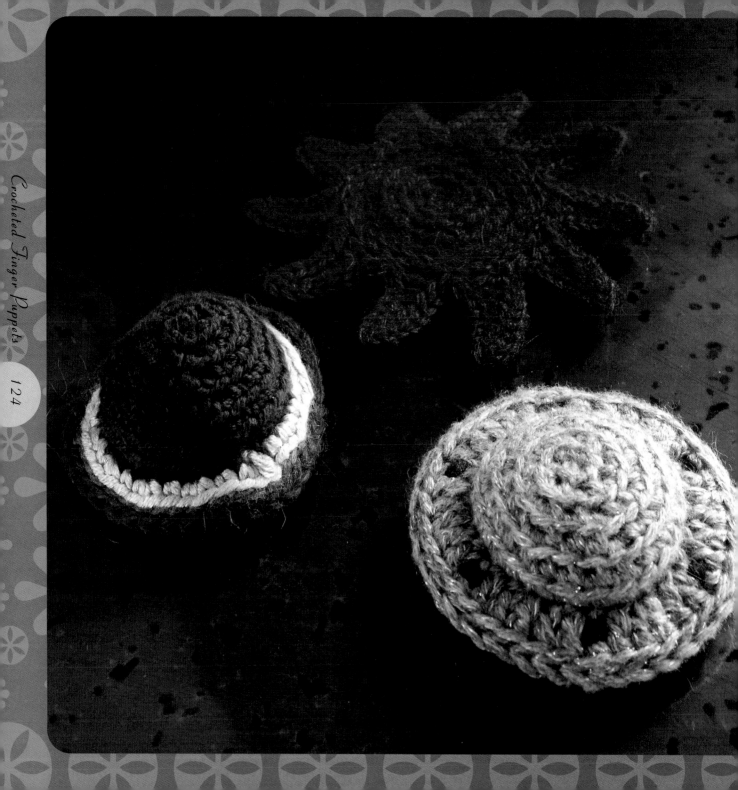

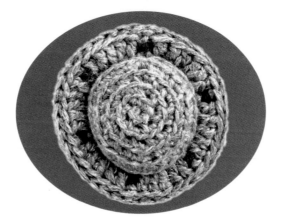

Five little men in a flying saucer flew round the world one day...
Make your own UFO, red giant star and world. Then whoosh
around the cosmos in your flying saucer!

UFO

Materials

- Any DK yarn in silver and red for UFO; red for star; any four colours for world
- 3.5mm (USE/4, UK9) hook
- Darning needle and scissors

Method

UFO: The This flying saucer starts as an inner piece wrapped with filler yarn. Then the outer piece is made and the two are stitched together. Finally, the yarn is rejoined to the middle and treble stitches worked for two rows, and then the outer edge of these two rows are joined with slip stitch.

Red giant star: The star is made from two centre pieces joined together. Rays are then worked outwards in rounds.

World: The world is worked in much the same way as the UFO, except for the optional rings.

For further guidance, see the branching out and turning back stitch diagram on page 149.

UFO

Work inner and outer pieces in spiral TBLs throughout inner and outer pieces.

Inner piece

With 3.5mm hook and silver yarn, mk floop and 1ch.

Rnd 1: 6dc into floop. 6 sts.
Rnd 2: Dc2inc 6 times. 12 sts.
Rnds 3–8: Wk even in dc.
Rnds 9–10: Wk even in ss.
Rnd 11: (1dc, dc2inc) 6 times. 18 sts.
Wk 2ss to finish. Fasten off.
Cut a length of 72in (180cm) silver yarn and wrap around inner piece loosely (as stuffing).

Outer piece

Rnd 1: 6dc into floop. 6 sts.
Rnd 2: Dc2inc 6 times. 12 sts.
Rnd 3: (1dc, dc2inc) 6 times. 18 sts.
Rnd 4: (2dc, dc2inc) 6 times. 24 sts.
Rnds 5–8: Wk even in dc.
Rnd 9: (1dc, dc2tog) 6 times. 18 sts.
Place inner piece inside outer piece.
Rnd 10: Ss2pcs tog to end.
Fasten off and sew in loose ends. *

Finishing

Working TFLs, rejoin silver yarn at rnd 6.
Rnd 1: Mk2ch, (1tr, tr2inc) to end.
Rnd 2: (1tr, tr2inc) to end.
Rnd 3: Ss2pcs tog (loosely).
Fasten off.
With darning needle and red yarn, sew on 'lights' here and there.

Red giant star

Work star in spiral TBLs throughout.

Centre back

With 3.5mm (US E/4) hook and red yarn, mk floop and 1ch.

Rnd 1: 6dc into floop. 6 sts.
Rnd 2: Dc2inc 6 times. 12 sts.
Rnd 3: (1dc, dc2inc) 6 times. 18 sts.
Rnd 4: (2dc, dc2inc) 6 times. 24 sts.
Rnd 5: (3dc, dc2inc) 6 times. 30 sts.
Wk 2ss loosely. Fasten off.

Centre front

Wk as for centre back but do not fasten off.
Put centre front and back tog with RSs facing outwards.
Rnd 6: Ss2pcs tog to last 5 sts, then, then work rem 5 sts as ss into front centre only (creating finger hole).

Rays

Rnd 7: ** (7ch, sk1ch, 1ss, 2dc, 2htr, 1tr, 1j-tr) for ray, then 1ss into next st of centre. Rep from ** to end. 10 rays. The rays will curl over as you make them on this row, but don't worry: this will be corrected by both the next two rows and by steam pressing during finishing.

Rnd 8: Ss around edge of rays, working (1ss, 1ch, 1ss) into each tip.

Rnds 9–10: Now ss two rnds right through the fabric between the centre and the rays.

Fasten off and sew in any loose ends.

Finishing

To encourage the rays to stay flat, lightly steam (if yarn is acrylic) or steam press (if yarn is a wool or cotton).

Variations

Try making a world in a variegated blue and white yarn (without the rings), to make an Earth-like planet.

World

With 3.5mm (US E/4) hook and any colour yarn, work as for UFO to *.

Finishing

Rings (optional)

With 3.5mm hook and working TFLs, join a contrasting colour yarn at rnd 6.

Rnd 1: Mk1ch, (1dc, dc2inc) to end. 36 sts.

Rnd 2: With a second contrast colour, ss (loosely) all around.

Rnd 3: With a third contrasting colour, ss (very loosely) all around.

Fasten off and sew in loose ends.

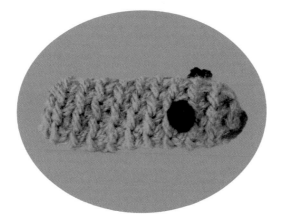

Where do space worms live? In a wormhole, of course!
As in all the best stories though, the wormhole leads to
an alternative reality – so be careful!

Worms

Materials

- Any DK yarn in any colour (plus black and red for eyes and mouth) for worm; blue and silver for wormhole
- 3.5mm (USE/4, UK9) hook
- Cardboard tube
- Darning needle and scissors

Method

Worm: These little worms are quick and simple to make, with simple tubular bodies. The eyes and mouth are then sewn on.

Wormhole: This is also reasonably easy to make, as it's just a bigger version of the tube-shaped worms with some embroidery to decorate.

For further guidance, see the basic body stitch diagram on page 148.

Worm

Wk in spiral TBLs throughout.

With 3.5mm hook and MC yarn, mk floop and 1ch.

Rnd 1: 6dc into floop. 6 sts.

Rnd 2: Dc2inc 6 times. 12 sts.

Rnds 3–10: Wk even in dc.

Rnd 11: Wk even in ss.

Wk 2ss to finish. Fasten off and sew in loose ends.

Finishing

With darning needle and black yarn, sew on eyes. With red yarn, sew on mouth.

Wormhole

With 3.5mm hook and blue yarn, mk
sl-knot and 30ch, and join with 1ss.
Wk in dc spiral TBLs for 30 rnds.
Wk 3ss to finish. Fasten off and sew
in loose ends.

Finishing

With darning needle and silver yarn,
do a little embroidery to add some
bling to your wormhole. Place
cardboard tube inside for structure.

Variations

*You could make googly crochet eyes
for your wormhole worms, using the
eye instructions from the Martian
puppet set in this book.*

Watch out for the evil Emperor Badguy! He dabbles in dark magic.
Monster minions to his right and rebellious robots to his left, he
is a force to be reckoned with.

Villain

Materials

- Any DK yarn in black and red
- 3.5mm (USE/4, UK9) hook
- Darning needle and scissors

Method

Make your villain's head first, and embroider the facial
features. The cloak is then made in one piece from the hood
down, working over the head and attaching it as you go.

*For further guidance, see the hooded cloak stitch diagram
on page 152.*

Villain

Work in spiral TFBLs throughout head and body.

Head

With 3.5mm hook and red yarn, mk floop and 1ch.
Rnd 1: 6dc into floop. 6 sts.
Rnd 2: Dc2inc 6 times. 12 sts.
Rnds 3–6: Wk even in dc.

Body

Rnds 7–17: Change to black yarn and wk even in dc.
Rnd 18: (1dc, dc2inc) 6 times. 18 sts.
Rnd 19: (2dc, dc2inc) 6 times. 24 sts. Finish with 2ss, then fasten off.
With darning needle and black yarn, embroider facial features and then set aside.

Cloak

Work in spiral TBLs throughout cloak.

Hood

With 3.5mm hook and black yarn, mk floop and 1ch.
Rnd 1: 6dc into floop. 6 sts.
Rnd 2: Dc2inc 6 times. 12 sts.
Rnd 3: (1dc, dc2inc) 6 times. 18 sts.
Rnd 4: (2dc, dc2inc) 6 times. 24 sts.
Rnds 5–7: 12ss (shaping hood above face), 12dc.
Rnd 8: 12ch (closing the hood under chin), sk 12 sts, 12ss.
Rnds 9–10: Wk even in ss.
Now put head/body inside hood and stitch into place.
Shoulders
Rnd 11: (Dc2inc, 11dc) twice. 26 sts.
Rnds 12–15: Work even in dc.

Cuffs

Rnd 16: * Dc2inc twice, 11dc, rep
from * once. 30 sts.

End cuffs

Rnd 17: (Sk5dc, 10dc) twice. 20 sts.
Rnds 18–21: Work even in dc.
Rnd 22: (1dc, dc2inc) 15 times. 30 sts.
Rnd 23: Wk even in dc.
Rnd 24: (2dc, dc2inc) 15 times. 45 sts.
Fasten off and sew in any loose ends.

Finishing

With darning needle, loosely stitch last
rnd of body to the inside of rnd 21 to
keep body in place, then weave in any
rem loose ends.

Variations

*You could make some minions for
Mr Badguy, using the monster
pattern in this book.*

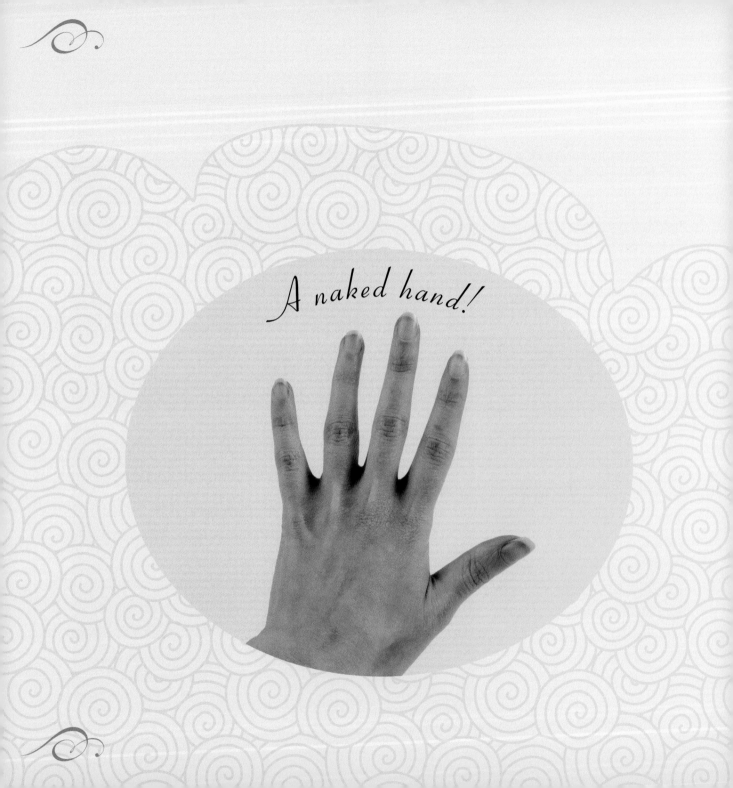

A naked hand!!

Techniques

How to make your fingers fabulous

Getting started

Tension swatches and sizing

When knitting or crocheting garments, testing that your tension (gauge) matches that given in the pattern is essential so that your finished project fits you properly. However, when making puppets your tension is not so critical. Make the inner body of your finger puppet first: if it fits your finger then your tension is just fine!

Buying yarn and hooks

If you have been knitting or crocheting for a while already, you probably have a stash of yarn just waiting to be transformed into finger puppets. All the designs in this book call for double-knit (DK) yarn, and I have used just two sizes of crochet hook throughout – 3.25mm (USD/3, UK10) and 3.5mm (USE/4, UK9). Use whatever yarns you have! I like to work with natural fibres; but for more economical puppets, acrylic is just fine too.

Branching out and turning back

This is a method I use frequently for shaping. For example, in the Octopus pattern the arms are made by 'branching out' with a series of chain stitches and then 'turning back' to work along the chain. See diagram on page 149.

TBL(s), TFL(s) and TFBL(s)

I use these terms frequently throughout the book. When you crochet a stitch, there are 2 loops on the top. TBL(s) means crochet Through Back Loop(s) only. TFL(s) means crochet Through Front Loop(s) only. TFBL(s) means crochet Through Front and Back Loop(s).

Following patterns

It's a good idea to read the pattern from beginning to end first, look up any abbreviations or terms if necessary, and gather all your materials together before starting to crochet.

Basic techniques

Holding the hook

There are various ways to hold your crochet hook. I hold the hook in the right hand (like a knitting needle) and feed the yarn from my left hand. Other people prefer to hold the hook like a pencil.

 Holding the hook.

 Feeding the yarn from the other hand.

Chain stitch (ch)

This is the most basic stitch.

 Loop yarn over hook.

 Pull loop through to form one chain stitch.

 Front view of chain.

Back view of chain.

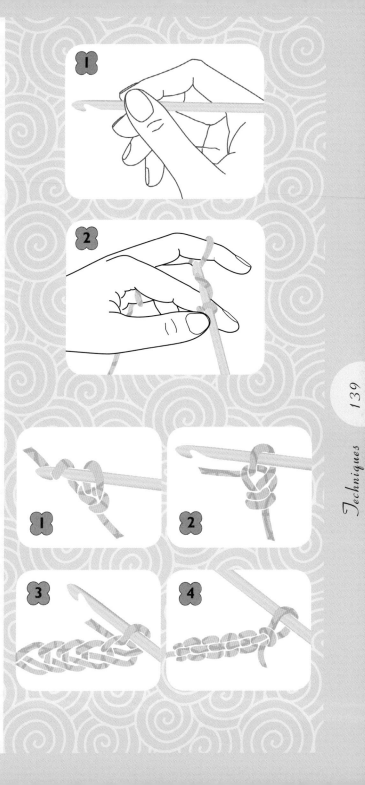

Slip stitch (ss)

This stitch is a neat simple stitch often used as an edging or where a very short stitch is needed.

 Hook through stitch, yarn over hook, pull through to finish off. 1 loop on hook.

 Continue in this way for required number of slip stitches.

Double crochet (dc)

This is the most common stitch used in this book. I often use it worked TBLs (through back loops) only, as this results in a lighter, more elastic fabric than when worked TFBLs (through front and back loops).

 Hook through stitch, yarn over hook, pull through stitch. 2 loops on hook.

Yarn over hook, pull through both loops to finish off. 1 loop on hook.

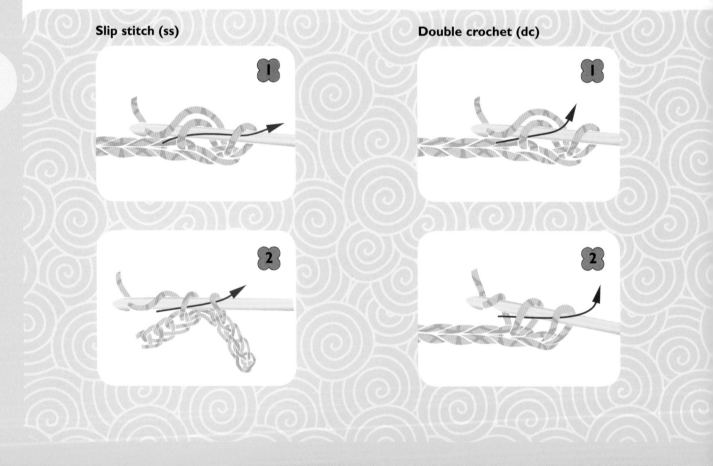

Slip stitch (ss)

Double crochet (dc)

Half treble crochet (htr)

This is a little taller than double crochet.

 Yarn over hook, hook through stitch, yarn over hook, pull through stitch. 3 loops on hook.

 Yarn over hook, pull through all 3 loops to finish off. 1 loop on hook.

Treble crochet (tr)

This is an even taller stitch.

 Yarn over hook, hook through stitch.

Yarn over hook, pull through stitch, yarn over hook.

Pull through 2 loops. 2 loops on hook.

Yarn over hook, pull through 2 loops to finish off. 1 loop on hook.

Double treble crochet (dtr)

This is the tallest of the stitches. Work as for treble crochet, shown above, but with one extra step (number 3, below).

Yarn over hook, hook through stitch.

Yarn over hook, pull through stitch, yarn over hook.

 Pull through 1 loop. 3 loops on hook.

 Pull through 2 loops. 2 loops on hook.

 Yarn over hook, pull through 2 loops to finish off. 1 loop on hook.

Half treble

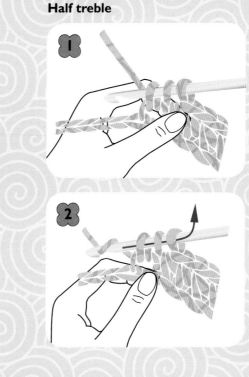

Treble crochet

Increasing

To increase, work multiple stitches into the next stitch.

Double crochet 2 to increase (dc2inc)
Work two double crochet stitches into the next stitch
(to increase by 1 stitch).

Double crochet 3 to increase (dc3inc)
Work three double crochet stitches into the next stitch
(to increase by 2 stitches).

Double crochet 4 to increase (dc4inc)
Work four double crochet stitches into the next stitch
(to increase by 3 stitches).

You will also see these sorts of increases worked in
half treble (htr2inc, htr3inc, htr4inc) and treble stitch
(tr2inc, tr3inc, tr4in).

Decreasing

To decrease a stitch, just work the first part of each of the
next two stitches, then finish them off together to make
them into one stitch.

Double crochet 2 together to decrease (dc2tog)

1 Hook through stitch, yarn over hook, pull through
stitch. 2 loops on hook.

2 Hook through following stitch, yarn over hook, pull
through stitch, yarn over hook.

3 Pull through all three loops to finish off. 1 loop
on hook.

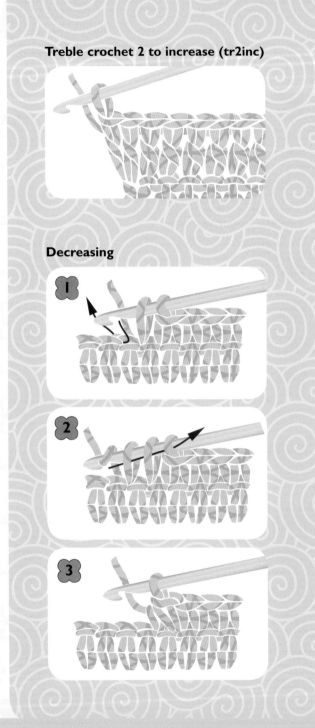

Treble crochet 2 to increase (tr2inc)

Decreasing

Half treble 2 together to decrease (htr2tog)

 Yarn over hook, hook through stitch, yarn over hook, pull through stitch. 3 loops on hook.

 Yarn over hook, hook through following stitch, yarn over hook, pull through stitch, yarn over hook.

 Yarn over hook, pull through all 3 loops to finish off. 1 loop on hook.

Treble 2 together to decrease (tr2tog)

 Yarn over hook, hook through stitch.

 Yarn over hook, pull through stitch. 3 loops on hook.

 Hook through following stitch, yarn over, pull through stitch. 4 loops on hook.

Yarn over, pull through 3 loops. 2 loops on hook.

Yarn over hook, pull through 2 loops to finish off. 1 loop on hook.

Decreasing multiple stitches

It is possible to decrease multiple stitches at once. For example, tr6tog means 'treble 6 together to decrease', making 6 stitches into one by working step 3 five times.

 Yarn over hook, hook through stitch.

 Yarn over hook, pull through stitch. 3 loops on hook.

 (Hook through following stitch, yarn over, pull through stitch) five times. 8 loops on hook.

 Yarn over, pull through 7 loops. 2 loops on hook.

 Yarn over hook, pull through 2 loops to finish off. 1 loop on hook.

Techniques

Spiral rounds (circular spiral)

This is begun with a foundation loop (floop), then worked in a continuous spiral with no joining slip stitches or turning chains. The right side (RS) is always facing.

Foundation loop (floop)

Yarn over hook twice, pull through to form loop, do not tighten as you will be working your first round (rnd) into this floop.

Rnd 1: Make 1 chain stitch (mk1ch), then work 6 double crochet stitches (6dc) into the floop. Pull beginning end of yarn to tighten the floop. Continue straight onto the next round, without making a join or turning chain.

Rnd 2: Work a dc2inc into each stitch of round 1. This is a typical beginning for the puppet pieces worked in spiral rounds.

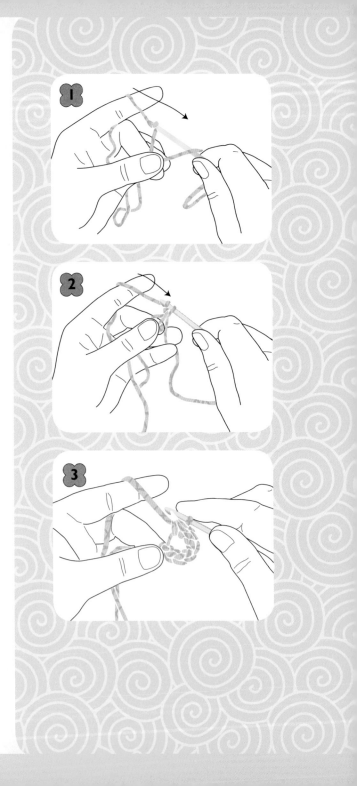

Relief stitches

These are a great way to add texture to your crochet. Rather than working into the tops of the stitches, you work around the middles instead.

Front post treble (fptr)

 Yarn over hook, hook under at middle of stitch.

 Yarn over hook, pull through stitch, yarn over hook.

 Pull through 2 loops. 2 loops on hook.

4 Yarn over hook, pull through 2 loops to finish off. 1 loop on hook.

Front post half treble (fphtr)

Work in the same way as the front post treble, but making a half treble stitch instead.

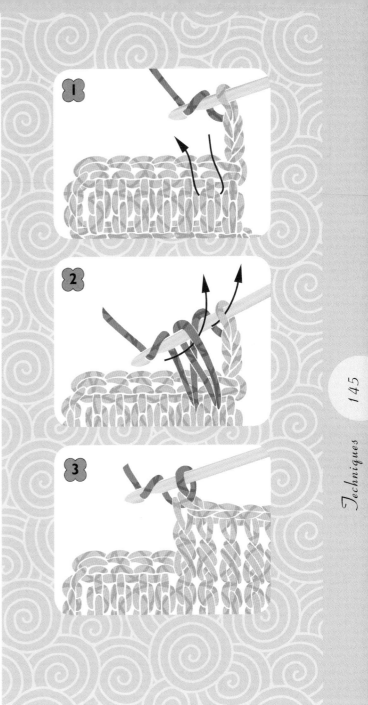

Joining stitches

These are great for joining pieces at a right angle. For example in the Octopus pattern you branch out and turn back to form each arm; then when you get back to the base you work this special stitch which joins it neatly. They are just like ordinary stitches but step 1 is worked into the side of the last double crochet stitch and step 2 works through the top of the next stitch of the previous round.

Joining double crochet (j-dc)

1 Hook through stitch, yarn over hook, pull through stitch. 2 loops on hook.

2 Needle through next stitch of previous round to join, yarn over hook, pull through all loops to finish off. 1 loop on hook.

Joining half triple crochet (j-htr) and Joining treble crochet (j-tr)

These are worked in the same fashion as the j-dc.

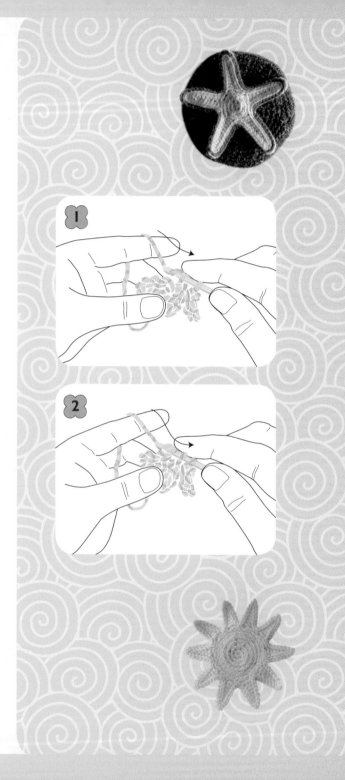

Finishing touches

Back stitch
So called because the stitches are worked backwards, from A to B, and then the needle emerges at C for the following stitch.

Mattress stitch
This produces a nearly invisible seam which is quite elastic.

Wrapping stitch
This is a handy way to hide unsightly stitching where body parts are joined. For example in the Penguin pattern I sewed on the flippers and then wrapped the sewing yarn around the join several times in order to make the join look neater, then sewed in the loose end as normal.

Double crocheting seams (dc2pcs tog)
Double crocheting two pieces together is an alternative to joining using a darning needle. Place the two pieces together and crochet each stitch right through both pieces at once.

Slip stitching seams (ss2pcs tog)
Work as for double crocheting seams but with slip stitch instead. This technique is used frequently in this book, usually to join inner and outer body pieces of the puppets.

Back stitch

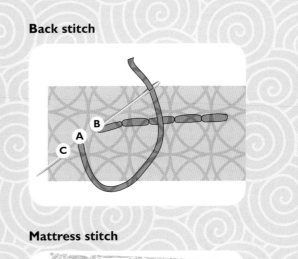

Mattress stitch

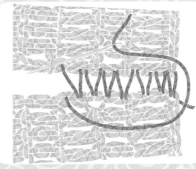

Double crocheting seams

Techniques

Stitch diagrams

꙼ Floop (foundation loop)

O Ch (chain stitch)

● Ss (slip stitch)

✕ Dc (double crochet stitch)

✕✕ Dc2inc (double crochet 2 into next stitich, to increase)

✕✕ Dc2tog (double crochet 2 together, to increase)

◤ Wk from the centre, outwards

1/2/3 etc Round/row number

FO Finish off

●● Ss2pcs tog (slip stitch 2 pieces together)

✖ Htr (half treble crochet stitch)

✖ Tr (treble crochet stitch)

✖ J-htr (joining half treble crochet stitch)

◥·. Shows the flow of stitches within a round/row

·. Shows how one stitch corresponds to another stitch on a following round/row

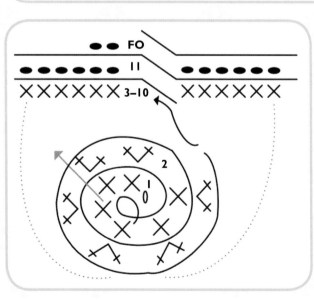

Basic body

This basic tube shape forms the body of the Bee, and the same concept is used for the inner bodies of many of the other puppets. The Worm body is almost identical to this (just one rnd shorter).

Start off as for the googly eyes but carry on straight to rnd 2, increasing to 12 sts. Work even in dc for the required number of rnds. Frequently the final rnd of the basic body is worked in ss to finish it off neatly, and in this case there are an extra 2 slip sts to finish off.

Rnd	Sts (inc/dec)
1	6
2	12 (+6)
3–10	12 (work even)
11	12

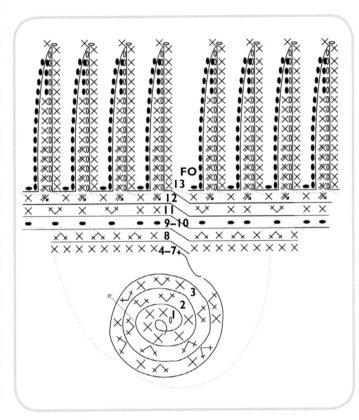

Branching out and turning back

This is a technique that's really handy for creating non-standard shaping. A good example is the Big Octopus, illustrated here.

Rnds 1–3 are worked like the outer body. You now have 18 sts. Rnds 4–7 are worked even in dc, rnd 8 decreases to 12 sts and rnds 9–10 are worked even in ss to draw the fabric in.

We are going to make 8 arms for the octopus; so we inc on the next rnd (from 12 sts to 16, so we have a number of sts divisible by 8).

Now we are ready to make the octopus' arms. * Mk15ch (this is 'branching out'). Then work back along the chain you just made (this is 'turning back'), by skipping 1 ch st first, then working 5ss, 5dc and 4htr along the rem 14 ch sts. Finally, make a j-htr followed by a dc into the base. Rep from * 7 times.

The next rnd finishes off the arms and body. Wk in dc up along the RH side of each arm, then (1dc, 1ch, 1dc) into each 'tip', and finally just ss back down along the LH side of each arm.

Rnd	Sts (inc/dec)
1	6
2	12 (+6)
3	18 (+6)
4–7	18 (wk even in dc)
8	12 (-6)
9–10	12 (wk even in ss)
11	16 (+4)
12	128 (+110)
13	144

Butterfly

1 We've illustrated here how the Little butterfly is made and put together. The Big butterfly is constructed on the same principles.

First, make a 10-rnd basic body, 6 polka dots (made just like the googly eyes) and the wings.

2 Next, sew two polka dots onto each of the upper wings, and one dot onto each of the lower wings. Sew the wings onto the sides of the body.

3 Finally, make the edging and antennae by slip-stitching all around. Start at the lower RH wing, ss around till you get to the head, make each antenna by working 1ss (8ch, sk1ch, 7ss), then work down around both LH wings. The actual number of slip stitches you need to make will depend on how you have sewn the wings on. This is not an exact science!

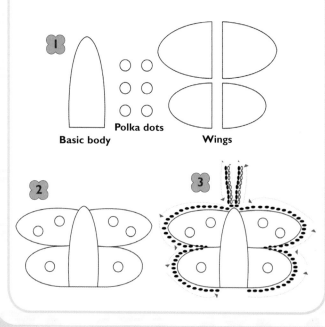

Basic body   Polka dots   Wings

Frog's legs

1 Froggie's back legs are made by working a sl-knot and 15ch first; then sk1ch, 4ss, 5htr, 5tr. Fasten off, leaving a tail for sewing.

2 Form the leg shape by folding, as shown below.

3 Sew onto the Froggie body, as shown below.

4 Froggie's front legs are even easier. Mk6ch, sk2ch, 1htr, 3ss.

5 Then sew each front leg onto the front of the body, just at the top.

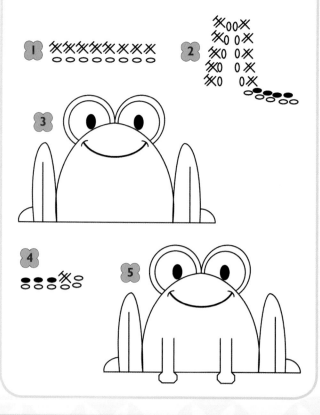

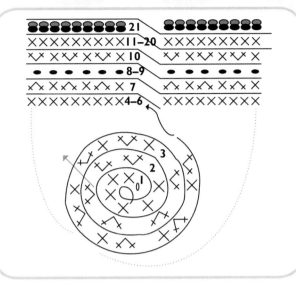

Outer body

Here is an example of an outer body; the Penguin. It is designed to fit over the basic body and the head is stuffed with a little extra yarn to give it padding.

Start off at the top of the head in the same way as for the basic body but add an extra round of incs (rnd 3).

Work even in dc for a few rnds, then dec to 12 sts again and wk a couple of rnds in ss to draw in the fabric for the neck.

We then inc to 18 sts again for the body and work rnds 11–20 even in dc.

Last but not least… the head is padded, the inner body placed inside and the two body pieces slip-stitched together (ss2pcs tog).

Googly eyes

Many of the characters in this book have googly eyes!

Start with a floop and 1ch, then wk 6dc into floop and finish with 1ss to join.

Rnd	Sts (inc/dec)
1	6

Rnd	Sts (inc/dec)
1	6
2	12 (+6)
3	18 (+6)
4-6	18 (wk even in dc)
7	12 (-6)
8-9	12 (wk even in ss)
10	18 (+6)
11-20	18 (wk evenin dc)
21	18 (ss2pcs tog)

Hooded cloak

There are two characters in this book that have cloaks; the Ninja and the Villain.

Both of these use a 'slit' technique which creates the open part of the hood, by making a chain which goes across a number of skipped stitches.

Here we have illustrated the Ninja cloak, including the hood 'slit'. The Villain's cloak is simply a slightly bigger version of this.

Wk rnds 1–3 in the same manner as the Outer Body.

Rnds 4–6 help to shape the hood, by working the first 9 sts in ss and then next 9 sts in dc.

Rnd 7 creates the hood slit. There is a little increase for the shoulders on rnd 10, then again on rnd 13 for the cuffs. The cuffs are finished off by simply skipping some stitches.

Rnd 17 doubles the number of sts, creating a flared hem; then a final rnd of ss is worked.

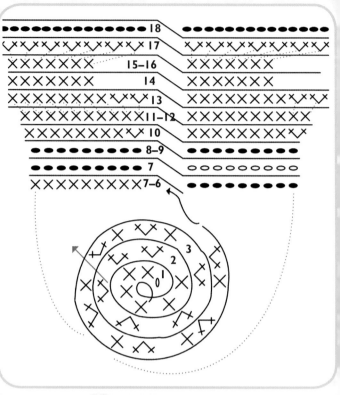

Rnd	Sts (inc/dec)
1	6
2	12 (+6)
3	18 (+6)
4–6	18 (wk even in ss/dc)
7	18 (slit rnd)
8–9	18 (wk even in ss)
10	20 (+2 for shoulders)
11–12	20 (wk even in dc)
13	24 (+4 for cuffs)
14	14 (-10 skipped cuff sts)
15–16	14 (wk even in dc)
17	28 (+14)
18	28 (wk even in ss)

Conversions

Crochet hook conversions

UK	Metric	US
14	2mm	B/1
13	2.25mm	–
12	2.5mm	C/2
11	3mm	–
10	3.25mm	D/3
9	3.5mm	E/4
8	4mm	G/6
7	4.5mm	7
6	5mm	H/8
5	5.5mm	I/9
4	6mm	J/10
3	6.5mm	K/10.5
2	7mm	–
0	8mm	L/11
00	9mm	M–N/13
000	10mm	N–P/15

Conversion of terms used

UK	US
Double crochet	Single crochet
Half treble	Half double crochet
Treble	Double crochet
Double treble	Triple crochet
Treble treble	Double triple crochet

Abbreviations

Approx	approximately		**Rnd**	round
Ch	chain, chain stitch		**RH**	right-hand side
CC	contrast colour		**RS(s)**	right side(s)
Dc	double crochet		**Sk**	skip
Dc2inc	double crochet twice in next stitch (to increase)		**Sl-knot**	slip knot
Dc2tog	double crochet two stitches together (to decrease)		**Spiral**	working in continuous rounds without joins
DK	double knitting (yarn)		**Ss**	slip stitch
Floop	foundation loop		**Ss2pcs tog**	slip stitch two pieces together
Fphtr	front post half treble stitch		**St(s)**	stitch(es)
Fptr	front post treble stitch		**TBL(s)**	through back loop(s)
Htr	half treble stitch		**T-ch**	turning chain
J-dc	joining double crochet stitch		**TFL(s)**	through front loop(s)
J-htr	joining half treble stitch		**TFBL(s)**	through front and back loop(s)
J-tr	joining treble stitch		**Tog**	together
LH	left-hand side		**Tr**	treble crochet stitch
MC	main colour		**Tr2tog**	treble crochet two stitches together (to decrease)
Mk	make		**Wk**	work
Rem	remaining		**WS(s)**	wrong side(s)

About the author

Gina Alton learned to knit and crochet at the age of five with help from her grandma Mildred and neighbour Ann. From this beginning grew a lifelong passion for all things yarny.

Now grown up (more or less), her working time is divided between pattern editing for *Knitting* magazine, writing about knitting and creating quirky crochet designs like the ones featured in this book.

Gina lives in the beautiful heart of Devon, England, with her children Allie and Fred... and her yarn collection, which seems to grow exponentially from year to year.

Creating beautiful and useful things with simply a hook or needles and some yarn is therapeutic, rewarding and enjoyable. Gina hopes you have as much fun making these puppets as she did designing them!

Main project photography: Laurel Guilfoyle
Cut out photography: Rebecca Mothersole
Pattern checking: Katrin Salyers

Index

Names of puppets are given in italics.

Contact us for a complete catalogue, or visit our website:
GMC Publications Ltd, 166 High Street, Lewes, East Sussex BN7 1XU, United Kingdom
Tel: +44 (0)1273 488005 Fax: +44 (0)1273 402866
www.gmcbooks.com